"A classic in astrological literature since its original publication in 2005, *Cycles of Light* brings the lens of depth psychology to illuminate one of the oldest astrological techniques and reveal its power as a centrepiece of astrological practice. Drawn from live teaching at the Centre for Psychological Astrology, the material is both practical and inspirational, weaving together a thorough understanding of method and detail with deep insight into human psychology. It is enriched by skilful and perceptive delineation of numerous solar return charts to show the range and potentials of this ancient technique.

As ever, Lynn Bell is here a masterly and assured voice. *Cycles of Light* represents the distilled wisdom of a lifetime practising and teaching astrology; it is essential reading for any student of astrology but just as equally valuable for experienced practitioners working with clients."

Carole Taylor
4th May 2022

Tutor and Ex-President of the Faculty of Astrological Studies and on the MA in Cultural Astronomy and Astrology at the University of Wales, Trinity Saint David

CYCLES OF LIGHT

EXPLORING THE MYSTERIES
OF SOLAR RETURNS

LYNN BELL

Raven Dreams Press
Boulder, CO

Published in 2022 by Raven Dreams Press
3980 Broadway Ste. 103 #186
Boulder, CO 80304
www.ravendreamspress.com

ISBN 978-1-7326504-4-2

Cover art by Simon Avery
Printed in the United States of America
LCCN 2022937664

ACKNOWLEDGEMENTS

In working on this seminar I have realised how many ideas from other people have gone into forming my own perspective as an astrologer. A whole generation of astrologers gave their ideas generously to us in our formative years, and they still do. I wish to thank that generation of teachers. And the students I teach, at the CPA, and elsewhere, for the wonderful discussions that inform my work. My gratitude to Stephen for his untiring support and patience, and the fine and discriminating eye he brings to the text. To Jules Cashford for conversations that inspired my imagination and fine-tuned my thinking. And to Liz Greene for creating such a delightful environment in which to work and publish.

TABLE OF CONTENTS

PREFACE

Here it is: a book on solar returns at last. For years, whenever I taught this material in France or Germany or England, someone would ask, "When are you going to write a book about solar returns?" The first seminar I taught at the CPA, in September 1995, was on solar returns. That tape fizzled, and the seminar that provides the kernel of this book was given nine years later, on 22 February 2004. I have added a great deal of material taught in other places at other times, in order to give the subject enough dimension, enough substance. I have also included an appendix with examples in the back, highlighting keys to interpretation. Solar returns can be enragingly obscure or marvelously to the point. I've tried to take the reader into the multi-chart dance, to show a number of ways to unravel their mysteries. This is not a cookbook, but if you try the dance steps you'll find a way into seeing these charts, and perhaps working with them. I hope that I've managed to communicate some of the excitement solar returns can give, and that the reader will be inspired to take another look, and another, and another.

The CPA was a wonderful place to teach. Liz Greene gave each of us free reign to choose our subjects, to work on what inspired us. She created an environment of mutual respect where astrology touched both intellect and soul, both mind and heart. Juliet Sharman-Burke was our administrating angel, unfailingly good natured and competent. I'm grateful to both of them. And I was always happy to have John Etherington's unique support in the back row of a seminar.

I'd like to thank Darby Costello and Yasmin Boland for reading through early drafts of some of this material, and all those whose stories have been graciously shared. Mark McDonough gave me the idea for the practical examples in the back of the book. I want to thank Yves Lenoble, Jean-François Berry, Luis Lesur, Karen Hamaker-Zondag, and Heidi Trier, and all who have all provided opportunities to teach this material in other cities and countries of the world. And for those of you who asked, I hope this is the solar returns book you've been waiting for. Thanks for asking.

Preface to the 2022 edition: This new edition of *Cycles of Light* has been patiently brought back to life by the persistence and skills of Tony Howard. I want to express all my gratitude for the gift of his time, his edits and his enthusiasm for this project. The original Centre for Psychological Astrology Press files were lost on a corrupted hard drive, and other backups were obsolete. It was no small task. To students new to solar returns, I hope you will find this volume as rewarding as its original readers did.

Lynn Bell, March 1, 2022

CHAPTER ONE

WHAT IS A SOLAR RETURN?

What is a solar return? It's as close as you can get to an astrological birthday chart, a chart cast for the moment the Sun returns to its exact natal position every year. We might imagine a solar return in the same way the seasons turn, the roses bloom, or the leaves fall from the trees. Yet everything has changed, since both the Earth and the Sun have been hurtling through space in their movement around the galactic center. The Sun becomes a prism through which we stop and look at how the planets have moved during the past twelve months, and how they join together at this moment of renewal in our personal cycle. How do these configurations come together inside of us? They are never the same; we never dip into the stream of stars again in exactly the same way. The solar return captures a moment in the cosmic dance for each of us, a moment that sheds light on the twelve months ahead.

For most people, a birthday is a natural time to think about the year to come, a time to pay attention. Each degree of the zodiac carries a particular stamp of solar energy, a unique quality that underlies our core sense of self. As the Sun returns to that degree, and even more precisely to the minutes and seconds of arc in our birth chart, that essential light is recharged, and each of the planets forms a new relationship to the Sun. Every time the Sun returns to its natal position, we are taking in a new piece of the larger universe, being asked to make it our own. Most of us experience our birthday time as special in some way. We may be weighing things, feeling time shift, closing a chapter on the recent past. At the same time, there is a sense that we hold the future in our hands. And a solar return is just that: a small piece of the future. Looking into it brings the rush of anticipation into play; using it together with transits and progressions opens up our understanding of the time ahead. There is a sense of renewal. It may already breeze in a few weeks before, bringing with it a feeling of warmth and hope, or the signs of storm and chill. At times, I've noticed the day itself has a particular quality, with events and conversations reflecting the year in miniature, like a day contained in a small sphere of glass.

Solar returns are an ancient technique, already mentioned in Firmicus Maternus. They fell out of use in England, and were then picked up again in the 20th century by sidereal astrologers. In France, however, they have been a central part of the astrological tradition, thanks in large part to the work of Alexander Volguine.[1]

---

1   Volguine writes that all the great Renaissance astrologers used solar returns. Nostradamus refers to them in his letters, and he cites Antoine de Villon and Junctinus of Florence as the sources for his approach. There is a huge difference in technique, however, since Junctinus calculated solar returns using profections. That is to say, the year after birth the natal 2nd house becomes the Ascendant; the following year it's the 3rd house that's placed on the Ascendant, and so on.

Why Isn't the Solar Return Always on the Birthday?

Audience: I've noticed that the solar return doesn't always coincide with a person's birthday, and I wondered if you could explain this.

Lynn: I'm sure you all learned this in beginner's astrology classes, but a day is not really twenty-four hours long; it's about four minutes less. Astrologers use something called sidereal time – literally, star time. A day is simply a turning of the Earth, even if our eye sees it as the Sun moving from east to west. As the Sun rises and sets, the circle of stars edges slightly forward each day. Our clocks and calendars are something of a fiction, but they work well enough until you wander into astrological territory. This small differential then adds up to nearly six hours every year, five hours and forty minutes to be exact, and accounts for the change in Ascendant from one solar return to the next. The Gregorian calendar added an extra day every four years: February 29, which realigns things until the system is tweaked again at the end of each century. If you think about it, you'll see that in a short time it can shift your solar return one day to either side of your birthday, since we are working with the moment the Sun reaches the same degree, minute and second in which it was placed at our birth. It can be confusing to see a solar return with the "wrong date," but the calendar is only a guide. Our real birthday, from an astrological point of view, is based on the Sun.

The Sun is the vital center of every chart, and its return lights up the year; it's a guide map, a light print, with clues for the next twelve months. We can do lunar returns, a Mars return, a Venus return, and each would have a particular focus, in keeping with the energy and qualities of the planet we choose as our starting point. But only the Sun brings a birthday chart. What does this new configuration reveal about the year to come? In my experience, it tells us a great deal about the kind of events and people, feelings and perceptions that will be with us in the next twelve months. The Sun can sometimes be a symbol for the small self, but it is also the source of light, of awareness. When we look at solar returns, we might wish to remember this larger dimension of the Sun.

I'd like to present an approach to solar returns that is perhaps slightly different than the ones you may be used to. Solar returns evolved as a predictive technique and were much favored by the tech-oriented sidereal school of astrology – valued or tossed aside to the extent that they 'fit' the events of the year, with little interest in psychological nuance. We will be looking at what may happen during the year ahead, but more importantly we'll be looking at how events come about, and what meaning they may have for us. This, too, is part of what a solar return chart reveals. Imagine looking through a kaleidoscope and turning the dial so that all those brightly coloured pieces of glass are rearranged into a new design. Solar returns show us how the pattern of the planets has changed in relation to something very specific – our natal Sun. These changes reflect inner experience as much as they reveal our 'real' world adventures. It may be possible to predict a move when a solar return has many planets in the 4th house, but this is only interesting if we can connect it to something inside the individual psyche. Selling a home, pulling up roots, is one way to choose a new identity, a new emotional base. And the space we live in says a great deal about who we are. The astrology we practice is always about enriching this dialogue between inner life and outer experience. Without it, we become mere technicians of banality. All of us are curious about the future and wonder what will happen in the year to come. Since psychological astrology has ambivalent feelings about prediction, it is interesting to come up against this frontier, where events begin to be perceptible and yet we are still primarily focused on how the soul pulls events into its path, and why.

SolaVision: What to Look For

First of all, look at the chart. Every solar return can stand on its own, and then we take a second look, comparing it to the natal chart. I don't know if any of you had the experience of going to the movies as a child and being handed a pair of 3D glasses. When you looked through the tinted cellophane, the image had added depth, extra dimension; it came more fully alive. Many students come to me with the solar return as a bi-wheel around the natal chart. Although this is a great technique for a second look, it is no way to look at a chart. You'll never see it!

James Eschelman wrote a book on solar returns in the 1970s in which he insisted that each solar return chart must be read twice - once as a chart in its own right, and the second in relation to the birth chart. I find this indispensable for working with solar returns. Some have energy of their own - strong aspects and angular planets - but very little connection to the birth chart. They can't be "seen" unless they are printed out as a separate chart. Other solar returns only reveal their meaning when you turn and check them in a detailed way against the natal positions; their meaning arises from a careful consideration of relationship to natal patterns and houses. You will need to move in and out of these two ways of seeing in order to work with solar returns. In many ways we are using basic interpretation skills, then adding extra layers, like the coloured film in those 3D glasses. We are weaving connections back and forth between two charts. Many fine astrologers have simply decided that solar returns aren't worth the extra effort, but I'll try to show you just how rich they can be.

Audience: What is the name of the book you mentioned?

Lynn: It's called *Interpreting Solar Returns*. Eschelman was a technical wizard, but also a siderealist, so he used a moving zodiac, and he advocated precessing the Sun, which I don't do.

You may remember that the ecliptic slips backwards against the fixed stars about 1° every 72 years. Like other sidereal and Vedic astrologers, Eschelman corrected charts for this movement by subtracting approximately 50 seconds from the Sun's position for each year. Over time there's a huge difference between the systems, and our zodiacs have drifted more than 23° apart in the past 2000 years. In solar return time, we shift a whole day in 72 years, so it's quite significant. Even though I don't use this technique, the book has many interesting points to make about solar returns, and I've integrated a certain number of them in my practice. It's not the only book that has inspired me. I used to mow through books and seize the ideas that seemed stimulating. At this point I'm not always sure where I first encountered certain ideas about solar returns! (See the bibliography for a list of books.)

Angular Planets in the Solar Return

If you're looking for action, you're probably looking at the angles of the solar return chart. Planets on the angles will be visible in the events and circumstances of the year, and they also describe our psychological orientation. The angles are powerful thresholds, with each marking a shift in our perspective. They are fixed by the exact time and place of the solar return, and each angle cuts the chart into a different quadrant. One of the reasons planets here are so significant is that they hold these strong places for such a short period of time, perhaps a half hour in every day – and in the solar return, conditions apply for one year. These planets have an acute, immediate quality. Notice that an exact birth time is a must if the solar return is going to work; it will quickly turn to mush if the birth time is off.

Any planet conjunct an angle in the solar return shapes the Sun's purpose for the year ahead. It's important to remember that these charts always have the Sun behind them – their whole meaning is derived from the Sun's position. If I say that Jupiter is conjunct the Ascendant in a solar return chart, it will open up our ability to express our solar identity through a Jupiterian filter. Now what happens when I say that? Even if you've never looked at a solar return before, you will already have ideas about what that might mean – you all have experience of the planets. Our brains have a primitive storehouse for keywords. When we hear Jupiter, words like "big," "lucky," or "good" are telegraphed to our neocortex, and we then turn them into something slightly more sophisticated.

Audience: You're right! "Success" just popped into my mind.

Lynn: The Ascendant is often described as our window on the world. If Jupiter is rising, the window is open wide. There will be a sense of buoyancy, of optimism, of confidence, and we could expect a general feeling of well-being, an openness to life and to others. Remember, though, this must later be layered over the natal chart, nuanced by what is found there. The extraverted signs will easily meld with an angular Jupiter, but more introverted signs like Virgo aren't suddenly going to be transformed into socialites. They would almost certainly enjoy the ease of contact with others but could find it more difficult to stay in their inner world, in their quieter places. With Jupiter rising, you are asked to bring what is inside out. This could come as an opportunity to show your best side to the world – the waves part, and the wind is at your back. There is less resistance to exchange with others. If Jupiter were on the Midheaven, it would bring a similar ease to stepping into a role in the world. It asks you to be bigger, to take on more, to allow yourself to take up space. Hmmm, I can hear the "abundance" keyword being activated in your minds.

Audience: I have a question about whether to calculate these charts for where I live, or for where I was born. The angles will change for different locations, won't they? And some people travel to a special place for their solar return. Which do you use?

Lynn: I use solar returns for the birthplace, but I do look at the relocated chart. I've brought some examples of this, which we'll look at in considerable detail later today.

Saturn Angular in the Solar Return

Lynn: Now, let's change gears, what would you expect with a planet like Saturn on the solar return Ascendant?

Audience: Seriousness, hard work. It could be a bit stuck.

Audience: Inhibition, frustration.

Lynn: All of this can be very true of Saturn. Even so, I think we must look more deeply into what Saturn asks of us. Saturn on any angle says, "Pay attention, this is no ordinary time." It may be a year of threshold crossing, of laying a foundation for many years to come; it comes with choice, maturity, *gravitas*. This is a year of consequence. It's helpful to remember that Saturn has a specific relationship to time; it takes us out of the world of absolute potential, into a moment that requires focus and seriousness, for a particular task, a particular purpose. And as astrologers, we are looking for a way to walk people through the year ahead, to connect them to this purpose. It is true that Saturn often brings increased responsibility, and this is always easier when we move into it willingly. Saturn narrows our choices, but our choices need to be narrowed at times. We only have to think of the Saturn return, and how much easier things get once we've made key decisions. It usually comes as relief not to be floundering any more.

Audience: Couldn't Saturn be a separating influence? I'm thinking of the sickle.

Lynn: Yes, that's true – in mythological terms Saturn cuts through a repressive system. Saturn always says, "The time has come." But the time for what? In the 1st house this might have to do with taking a stand and accepting the feeling of loneliness that comes from walking away from an old identity, from separating out. Saturn is often helpful for young people, who need to step into their own skin, to claim what they are and what they are not.

Of course when we are working with myths, there are always multiple possibilities, and Saturn can also be the tyrant, the one who swallows his own children. Saturn can bring us up against conditions in the outer world that seem difficult, even daunting, but these conditions arise in order to help us define who we really are. On the Midheaven it can bring authority figures into play – parents, teachers, supervisors, directors – but it can also kick up our fear of responsibility, our fear of making mistakes, our reluctance to take on a particular task. It can force us to confront our unwillingness to be the one who makes the decisions, to incarnate authority. Saturn can have that feeling of, "Oh, no, here we go again." But we are in fact being measured to the highest standard, a standard that obliges us to move beyond our fears and limitations. When this is not possible, or when our fear is too great, it can feel crushing.

Audience: You're saying that Saturn isn't so difficult.

Lynn: Astrology teachers spend a lot of time trying to keep people from getting trapped by fear of Saturn. We're not dissimulating, either. It takes some time to see the incredible gifts that Saturn brings, without necessarily denying that it can be a difficult and lonely process.

Natal and Solar Return Planets in the Same Degree

There are times when Saturn corresponds to very difficult situations. I was a bit perplexed reading for a Leo client in 2002, a year which promised many Jupiter transits, but Saturn was on the solar return Ascendant. It also happened to be conjunct the degree of the natal Moon.

Audience: Does that mean that Saturn was transiting the Moon?

Lynn: Yes. Notice that here I'm integrating information from another level, referring the solar return back to the birth chart. And it also meant that, of the two transits, Jupiter-Sun and Saturn-Moon, Saturn was likely to be the more dominant one. This is in fact what happened. His elderly mother was diagnosed with cancer and given six months to live. So he began to spend an hour or two with her every day after work, visiting her in the nearby retirement community where she'd moved a few years before to be close to her only child. Notice that all the Saturn-Moon symbolism is present: elderly woman, family responsibility, caring for his mother in difficult circumstances. Not long after, his wife began to have horrible symptoms. She was often in pain and had been taken to the hospital and dismissed without cause several times. It later turned out that she had an infection in the spine eating away the bone. He began to feel that work was the only place of refuge. And indeed he was given a substantial raise. But he could never take his eyes off all that he had to do. Uranus was on the Midheaven of the solar return, by the way, and trine Saturn.

Audience: Freedom through work.

Lynn: Absolutely – but a very narrow range of it. Now, this was a man who had felt almost no emotional connection to his mother as a child. He wasn't particularly interested in family, and he acted primarily out of a sense of duty. But in doing so, he slowly broke through the sense of disconnect he'd always had with his mother.

Audience: It sounds as though he was forced to heal something.

Lynn: He wasn't forced to visit his mother every night. He was the one who chose to be so assiduous in his visits. And his mother didn't die; she had several "miracle" recoveries. So his time of exquisite and constant attention lasted beyond this solar return. It's true that Saturn set up an extremely difficult situation, but he took it on in a very specific way.

Audience: I'm struck by how Saturn actually brings a lunar connection because it's on the Moon's degree. It functions like a conjunction.

Lynn: I would describe it as a focus; the natal planet comes through this focus into the chart. This happens whenever a solar return planet is near the degree of a natal planet: it becomes a conduit for that natal energy. I think it's clear that Saturn on the degree of the natal Moon reawakens the past through external difficulty of some kind. The Moon comes through duty, and duty leads, oddly enough in this case, to more feeling, to an integration of the past, to genuine relationship. In his case the solar return gave fundamental information about the year ahead.

The Moon Angular in the Solar Return

Audience: I am noticing that my sister had Moon on the Ascendant in the solar return last year, when she had a child. It's so appropriate from a symbolic point of view. Is that typical?

Lynn: I've often found the Moon to be strong in the charts of pregnancies. Saturn can be powerful as well. I think the reasons are obvious; both these planets have to do with parenting, and something long-term is being set in motion. No two individuals experience the same event in the same way. A first pregnancy isn't the same as a third, and the outer event finds its place in the individual's psyche in different ways. So don't expect the Moon to always be potent in these charts.

Audience: Would you counsel someone with an angular solar return Moon to have a child?

Lynn: It might very well happen on its own! The Moon has an ancient connection to fertility. We associate the Sun with creativity, but the Moon brings life-giving moisture, and in most cases this fecundity is psychological, metaphorical. Of course there are many ways an angular Moon might be expressed; it works to enhance the inner life. Our feeling nature wakes up, our soul stirs, and we find ourselves drawn to those who embody these qualities, who light up an obscure part of our own nature. The Moon can evoke a need for protection, for caring, for closeness. It softens the edges of our world, bathes it in a gentler light.

Audience: Would the Moon bring changes in the actual relationship with the mother?

Lynn: Yes, of course, that's one of the possibilities. I'm thinking of an example where the Moon was in the 4th, although rather far from the IC, close to the 5th. It was the solar return chart for a woman with a difficult family situation, and the Moon in the solar return was in opposition to Jupiter and trine Venus. What could be described by the opposition to Jupiter?

Chart features (Lorna):
- Ascendant at 9° Virgo trine Venus at 3° Taurus
- Moon at 4° Capricorn trine Venus and the Ascendant
- Moon at 4° Capricorn conjunct Chiron at 12° Capricorn
- Jupiter at 7° Cancer sextile Venus and the Ascendant
- Moon-Chiron opposite Jupiter

Audience: Could this have to do with travel? With stepping over the boundaries into something new?

Lynn: I like that description. Jupiter opens things up. The opposition to Jupiter releases the feelings of the Moon, feelings that can range from uncomfortable to jubilant. The Moon was in Capricorn, not a sign known for exuberant emotions, and conjunct Chiron, so this combination could be a reminder of past frustration, but equally an invitation to open up and to heal.

Audience: Moon-Chiron in the 4th feels painful to me. I wonder if there was a health problem for one of her parents?

Lynn: In this case the Moon-Chiron in Capricorn had to do with a pattern of withholding and distance. It described a situation where the mother never called her children or asked how they were, and so Lorna had stopped calling. At the time of the solar return, she hadn't spoken to her mother in several years, and a small crisis in the family made her pick up the phone. To her surprise, she found her mother more affectionate and engaging and, without meaning to, re-established a connection, and found her mother had changed.

Audience: Didn't Mark Twain say something about how stupid he'd found his father when he was seventeen, and how wise he'd become when he turned twenty-one?

Lynn: Yes, that's right, although this woman was considerably older. She had been angry with her mother for years, and she said that the anger simply evaporated. It was gone, finished, done with. Of course she'd been in therapy for quite a while, so that may have had something to do with it! Still, the prevalence of trines in the solar return immediately tells us of this potential for healing, for integration.

The Moon in this chart forms a grand trine with the Ascendant and Venus. Harmonious aspects like these to the Moon suggest a real possibility of emotional integration, and the 4th house is the natural home for the Moon, bringing out its connection to family, to the personal past. Whether this takes place in our actual relationship with a parent or inside our own psyche is an interesting question. Remember, we carry our parents within us long after they leave this world; our memories of them as young and vibrant, or angry and frightening, are alive in our psyches, and often healing has to do with working on the distortions in these inner images. I know I haven't given you the complete chart, but I'd like to add one more piece of information. If we overlay the solar return planets onto the natal chart, we get an additional layer of meaning. In this case the solar return Moon was in opposition to natal Uranus. Its solar return position filled in the empty space in a natal T-square.

This means it was carrying quite a potential for conflict, for explosive events, or for change. The solar return aspects give a field that modifies and adapts this potential. In this case it was warming and gentle, but I doubt this would have been the case if the Moon were affected by strongly dissonant aspects. Here the Moon is picking up an entire planetary structure. This individual has Sun-Uranus in the birth chart, and we know that Uranus can cut off from others, can seek to live outside of ordinary contact, perhaps in an intellectual world, in a faraway place that others can't reach. This distancing can be even stronger when both Saturn and Uranus are involved. She has an acute sense of herself as different from others. Here we could say that the Moon is confronting this tendency to disconnect, but it is the harmonious structure between solar return planets that tells us this will be lived with grace – or that there is at least an opportunity to do so.

Additional chart features (Lorna):
- Solar return (SR) Moon opposite natal Uranus
- Natal T-square: Sun opposite Saturn, Sun and Saturn square Uranus
- SR Moon fills the empty space of the natal T-square (opposite Uranus)
- SR Moon square natal Sun
- SR Moon square natal Saturn

Audience: How would you interpret the link to the natal pattern, then?

Lynn: As I said before, the Moon picking up the natal T-square is carrying a lot of tension. It would be easy to imagine this as an indicator for conflict, for a possible crisis. And this did happen: the conflict was over money issues. In this case the Moon softened the structure; it took the edginess away, and it allowed this woman to relax – never easy for someone with Sun opposition Saturn and square Uranus.

Audience: I suppose a strong Moon in the solar return could be uncomfortable for anyone, man or woman, who hasn't developed the feeling function.

Lynn: What a good way of putting it! As most of you know, an undeveloped part of the psyche often magnetizes circumstances or people into our lives so that we can grow in that very direction. But initially it may feel very unfamiliar. You might read something to the effect that the Moon angular in the solar return could indicate a year where "women play an important role in the life of the native." This would be one way to begin to integrate the feelings represented by the Moon.

Audience: Wouldn't that be more likely with the Moon on the Descendant?

Lynn: It might seem that way, although the real difference is probably more a question of perspective. It feels more "outside" in the 7th house and more "inside" on the Ascendant. Both placements can bring important people into our lives.

Audience: I'm not sure I understand exactly. Would this mean that a woman who has a baby would be more aware of her own feeling experience with the Moon on the Ascendant, but if the Moon were on the Descendant she'd see the emotions as coming from the child? Is that what you're saying?

Lynn: Something like that, although these processes are so subtle, they can't always be perfectly calibrated, they shift back and forth, especially with the Moon. Think of it as a dynamic that can be set into motion during the Solar Return – a planet on the Descendant is always in relationship with the Ascendant axis – they work together. In fact the image that just popped into my mind is classically Libran – imagine holding the scales in your hand and placing an object on one side.

Audience: The other side reacts.

Lynn: Yes. And usually there's a response to bring things into balance. This is how the Ascendant/Descendant axis works. You can also think of it as a way to understand oppositions. In the example you just gave, the descendant could symbolize an emotional shift in the partnership, around the birth of a child.

Audience: Ah, that makes sense!

Lynn: Imagine how strong a placement like that could be for someone who has all their planets in the east natally, on the Ascendant side. Moon in the 7th in the solar return could open a window to the mysterious inner workings of other people. Then again, they might suddenly start channeling our mothers!

Audience: Oh, No!

Pluto Angular in the Solar Return

Audience: How could you balance out something like Pluto?

Lynn: It's not easy, since Pluto has such a strong impact. You usually have to spend some time going into Pluto's territory before you come out again. It could feel completely out of balance.

Audience: Could Pluto rising correspond to a sense of invisibility?

Lynn: I like that idea – some aspect of the individual is out of sight, invisible to others, and yet there's a feeling, a Pluto field that is unmistakable, as if weight and gravity changes.

Audience: If it's anything like a Pluto transit to the Ascendant, then the person will never be the same! I see what you mean about time, though. I felt my Pluto transit lasted for years, but that wouldn't be the case in a solar return.

Lynn: Solar returns are concentrated opportunities; in some ways they are very specific. I'd say that any outer planet on the Ascendant opens a door for a brief period of time. I remember a fairy tale I read as a child. The hero is on a quest and tries to follow some mysterious intruders, but they always disappear without a trace. Then one night, under the right phase of the Moon, some elaborate writing appears on the wall of a mountain. When the words are pronounced, a hidden door appears. An outer planet is a bit like that – it gives us access to a dimension that we know exists, but it becomes available only at the right time. What is distinctive about the Ascendant is that it has to do with personal identity. With Pluto here in the solar return chart, individuals sometimes step away from an old identity. It can bring a sense of strangeness; you look in the mirror but someone else is looking out at you, a stranger in a strange land. I have often seen this aspect present when an old sense of self is ripped away. It can happen through a major move, through pregnancy, through leaving a career, or through psychotherapy. Sometimes there is a sense of pressure, a heavy atmosphere without any significant outer change; but it is rare to find a year without a major shift in identity when Pluto is so strong.

Audience: This combination of Pluto and the Ascendant feels like a birth of some kind. Of course birth and death are close together. And often people resist change, and then Pluto is heavy, oh so heavy.

Audience: If Pluto were in the opposite house, on the Descendant, could it still affect self-image?

Lynn: Yes, absolutely. It is in aspect to the Ascendant, after all, but the process is slightly different. Other people close to us might start acting in strange, uncomfortable ways. We may meet someone or experience something in others that wakes up this strangeness. At times this will seem to come out of nowhere, to be completely unrelated to our sense of self. But again the real question may be, where does "I" end and the other begin? It does of course sometimes happen that fate walks into our life via other people, and Pluto on the Descendant in a solar return could certainly describe a moment like that.

Audience: Could Pluto on the 7th house cusp in a solar return activate some experience of the shadow? I don't know how to express it exactly, but I have a feeling it is still related to something inside the person.

Lynn: That's a helpful way to think about it. Most of you are aware that, of all the houses, the 7th seems to be a lightning rod for projection. All of us see the world through the filter of our own psyche. The more we are involved emotionally, the more expectations we have, the greater the tendency to project a piece of ourselves onto an outside situation. This means that if you have Jupiter in the 7th house natally, you are predisposed to seeing your partner as wonderful. That's great for them, but it may not be for you. Your partner is good and wise and understanding, or they are wildly successful, or they could become the teacher or the spiritual authority in the relationship. It sounds good, but it can set up an imbalance. If they know more or better than you do, where then is your own wisdom? This is what is meant by projection – a piece of your own psyche comes back to you from outside. All of us project; it's one of the ways we learn. We sit up and take notice when someone fits our inner picture.

Pluto often represents parts of us that remain unknown, and therefore fascinating or frightening. So I think you are right in speaking of the shadow, the disowned and unacknowledged elements of the psyche. The shadow can crop up in many other places in a chart, so do keep that in mind. Pluto may test our feelings of power or powerlessness in relationship to others.

Audience: What if Pluto is in the 7th but not conjunct the cusp? Does all this still apply?

Lynn: The general theme is there, of course. One of the reasons we've begun by talking about angular planets is that they are one of the strongest indicators in a solar return. Their presence will be obvious in the way the year unfolds, and they are more likely to correspond to events, or to years of significant change. This influence, while still present, becomes much less powerful once a planet is off the angle. Of course we're assuming that we're working with an accurate birth time. Remember, that's an important consideration.

Audience: By angular, do you mean a five-degree orb?

Lynn: I would go up to eight degrees, perhaps a bit less for the 6ᵗʰ house. The general rule in astrology is that the tighter the aspect the stronger it is, but in solar returns there is more flexibility, and this partly depends on the strength of the planet. And we may observe an effect as far as twelve degrees (one degree per month). We'll explore the reasons for this a little later.

An Example of Angular Planets

Let's look at a solar return where quite a few planets are angular. Let's see what information we can find in the return chart alone; we'll look at the birth chart later. What do you first notice about this chart?

Audience: It looks very strong. Saturn is rising and opposing a Pluto-Mars conjunction on the Descendant. It looks like some kind of extreme tension.

Audience: There's got to be a struggle going on, a major conflict in relationship. Could this be the solar return of a divorce?

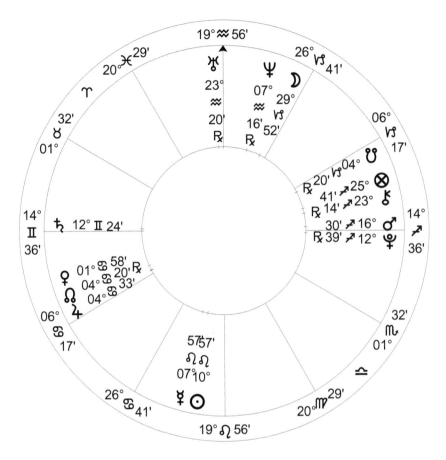

Martha Stewart
Solar return for 2001, set for birthplace

Lynn: Let's slow down a minute. I think we're caught up in the intensity of the chart, which comes through so strongly. First, let me point out a couple of things. Everyone on Earth had Saturn opposition Pluto in their solar returns during either 2001 or 2002. This reflects our participation in a collective process that came to be codified as 9/11. We were witnesses to a change in the structure of the world, most strikingly when the towers of the World Trade Centre collapsed. These energies become personal in this solar return because of the connection to the Ascendant/

Descendant axis. We could say that something built into relationships with others has reached a point of maximum tension.
A divorce might describe that, but so would a hostile takeover
in business, or a lawsuit, or a relationship in crisis. Our task as
astrologers is to give people ways to work with the energies that
will come up in the year ahead, how to avoid pitfalls, or how to
prepare for change. But even more, as psychological astrologers
we wish to understand the internal processes that correspond to
external events. Let's see if we can interpret the chart in that way.

Scandal and Power: Uranus and Pluto

Audience: I am noticing the contrast between Mars and Pluto
on the 7th house cusp, which feels challenging, even hostile, and
the Venus-Jupiter conjunction in the 1st house. These seem contradictory, to say the least. There's attraction and repulsion.

Audience: Uranus is on the Midheaven, so if there is a conflict,
it might lead to a change, a shake-up in career. Other people are
pushing her to change, acting strangely. We've just been speaking about that with Pluto on the Descendant. With Saturn rising,
she's trying to control.

Audience: There's a power struggle – a struggle to get others to
see her point of view. And yet Venus-Jupiter is a charm offensive.
She's got a lot going for her. Saturn in Gemini, though – something about communication and responsibility.

Lynn: I think you have a good sense of the central issues in the
chart. Let's look closer at the issues around communication.
With Saturn conjunct the Ascendant from the 12th house side,
we may be looking at a pattern of miscommunication that has
been building for some time. This is consistent with our usual
12th house interpretations. It may be important to stress that

something could be overlooked, that she is likely to have serious differences of opinion with other people. The possibility for mis-understanding is extremely high. Mercury rules the Ascendant here, and it's in an exact opposition to Neptune, saying the same thing in even more emphatic symbolic language. This is a classic aspect of misjudgement, of believing what you wish to believe, of self-deception. Neptune brings us into the territory of dreams and possibility, but it isn't concerned with objective reality. It's wonderful for artistic inspiration, but may not be terribly helpful in business. And yet, with Saturn rising she may begin the year feeling perfectly in control.

Audience: Perhaps we're seeing a huge change brought about by 9/11, a change beyond the control of any individual.

Lynn: That's part of it, I'm sure, but there's a very personal story here as well. I'm assuming you all know who Martha Stewart is? She built a home decorating and cooking empire based on her very real talents, her blonde composure, and hard work. Her television programs had a huge following. This is the solar return for Martha Stewart the year she was accused of insider trading – selling her stock on a tip that the owner was selling his. I suppose we could see Pluto in the 7th as outside temptation, but also as the very public outcry against her, the shadowy fascination that comes from any media mob lynching. Many people see her as a scapegoat, someone who got caught for what everyone was doing. Uranus on the MC did indeed bring a shock to her professional life. Her stock dropped 13% the day after she was indicted, she had to withdraw as CEO of her company, and her image and reputation have been battered. Let's see what the natal chart says about this, and how it connects to the solar return.

Here is Martha Stewart's birth chart. This is a fiery chart backed by a great deal of earth. She dazzled audiences with perfect cooking, an impeccable home, tasteful designing; she became the Queen of Home Arts, with Sun in Leo and Venus in Virgo high in the chart.

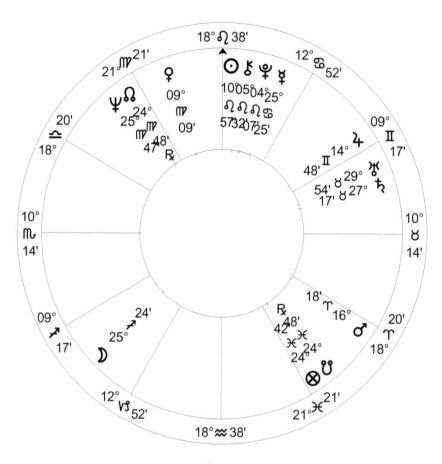

Martha Stewart
Natal Chart
August 3, 1941, 1:33 EDT, Jersey City, New Jersey

Audience: I think she was called the diva of domesticity! It strikes me as a very wilful chart – Scorpio rising, Sun conjunct Pluto, and Mars in Aries in the 5th house. There's more here than just sewing talent.

Audience: I remember reading that she has very little time for people who don't work as hard as she does, that she's very demanding, very perfectionist. Chiron-Sun must have been involved in what happened to her.

Lynn: Perhaps it is her desire for perfection that got her into trouble. There's always something fascinating about people who do everything well, who never have a hair out of place. They seem favored by the gods, and admired by others who are secretly waiting for them to drop the plates. And Venus in Virgo rules her 12th house. Julia Child, another Leo Sun who cooked in front of the cameras, was famous for her gaffes and wacky humor. In Martha Stewart's chart, the strong 9th house aims for the divine, and Leo aims for excellence. I'm thinking of another minor deity with Pluto-Sun conjunct in Leo – Arnold Schwarznegger, who became Mr. Universe, the husband of a Kennedy, and now governor of California.

Audience: Not to mention the Terminator!

Lynn: Martha has the Midas touch. This is a quote I found in *Slate* magazine:

> Martha has proved that alchemy is not impossible: Brush enough gold paint on enough flora, and eventually you'll make real gold. Tuesday's initial public offering for Martha Stewart Living Omnimedia – Omnimedia, has there ever been a more perfect name? – killed on Wall Street, rising from $18 to $52 before settling at $36. She arrived at the stock exchange that morning toting a tray of brioches. She left that evening holding $1.2 billion (in stock, not dough).[2]

---

2   "Martha Stewart: She's a Good Thing", by David Plotz, posted Friday, October 22, 1999, at 6.00 pm PST.

I'm struck by the mythical elements here: the writer's association to gold and alchemy, the Plutonian verb "killed," even Omnimedia – all reflect the Pluto-Sun conjunction in her chart. Her brioche turns to gold! When we touch the realm of the gods, there is always the accompanying danger of *hubris*. Aiming for perfection may be admirable, but it's also dangerous if you step off the path. Stewart is the classic self-made American whose drive and determination, and ability for self-promotion, made her unimaginably wealthy. Her chart fits classical astrological ideas of great wealth, with the natal Moon in the 2nd house in Sagittarius and the house ruler, Jupiter, in the 8th. You will notice that she has four planets in the 9th house, a house of strong beliefs, which we also connect to ethical issues and legal judgements.

There is very little doubt that Martha believes in herself and her abilities. Perhaps more than any other house, the 9th is about truth and self-knowledge, and Sun-Chiron-Pluto here may indicate a lack of ethical wholeness, or even more simply, a fallible vein running through the godlike expectations of this placement. Perhaps having so many planets in this exalted, idealized house makes the boomerang of ethical lapse even harder to deal with. The solar return we're looking at, so close to the Neptune opposition Sun transit, marks the beginning of a fall from grace, with legal battles to continue for several years. She was being told that she isn't who she thought she was, and we know that these transits can be profoundly troubling for personal identity.

Audience: I notice she has the Moon in aspect to Neptune in the birth chart – they're square, so how would that affect things?

Lynn: Moon in Sagittarius square Neptune in the birth chart also feeds into an outsized vision of herself. It could describe an emotional identification with her image, with the television Martha. It is very difficult not to be absorbed into the myth of one's own celebrity, especially when Neptune is powerful. But this can result in an inflation of certain aspects of the psyche, while others dry up. Neptune in transit has a reputation for disillusionment, but it is precisely this kind of false self that's acted upon. It is very painful, but it is also an opportunity to contact the real feelings that often lie hidden under the magical construction.

Audience: Pluto will soon go over the degree of the Moon and square Neptune. Is that more of the same? It looks to me like a change in values, with Pluto coming up to those degrees by transit. Perhaps it could wake up the compassion of Moon-Neptune, or bring the beginning of a new direction, more spiritual values.

Lynn: You may be right. The newspapers made a lot of jokes about Martha redesigning the prisoners' uniforms. It's likely that Uranus on the 10th was about moving her onto a new path in life. She's now been through the Neptune oppositions to Sun-Chiron and Pluto, and the Queen was pulled down in the eyes of the masses. And yet this is a very strong chart, with a great capacity for regeneration. We'll have to wait and see. Let's go one step further and place the solar return planets around the natal chart. What do you see?

Audience: The solar return Ascendant is in the 8th house, which makes sense since it is about debt and money. So many planets fall in the money houses, the 2nd and the 8th!

Audience: It looks like the Ascendant is exactly conjunct natal Jupiter. I would expect that to be fairly positive, so I'm feeling confused.

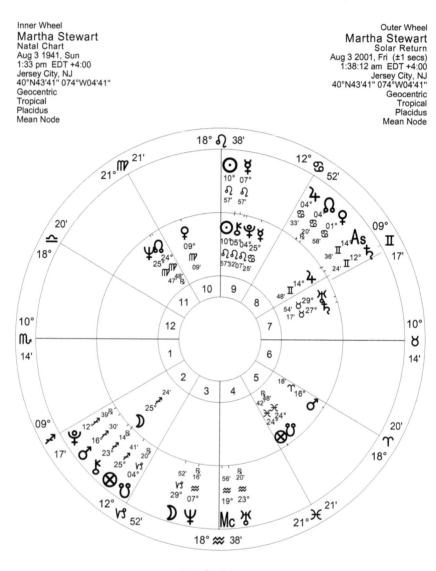

Martha Stewart
Inner wheel: birth chart
Outer wheel: solar return for 2001

Lynn: In traditional astrology, Jupiter is not at its best in Gemini. It might even be a signature for some sleight of hand, for some minor dishonesty. Under ordinary circumstances, I think this would be a favorable indicator, but not with Saturn and Pluto a few degrees away. The 8ᵗʰ house often brings about crisis; it carries the symbolism of the fall through analogy with the Sun bending down towards the western horizon. The Greeks thought of it as one of the entrances to the underworld, and Martha Stewart has a natal Sun-Pluto conjunction, a signature for that archetypal downward journey, the battle between dark and light. Jupiter is the ruler of her 2ⁿᵈ house, and as you've pointed out, all this is about money; it's the territory where the battle takes place. Notice that the Midheaven is also opposite its natal position, pulling energy away from the outer world, away from career, toward the deepest resources of the self.

Audience: We haven't spoken much about the Moon. I notice that it's void of course, and in a difficult sign, Capricorn, and also opposing natal Mercury and natal Pluto.

Lynn: I'm glad you mentioned the Moon, because it is often the most important indicator in a solar return. I do think it's significant that the Moon is at the very end of the sign. Something is coming to an end. We could see it as the culmination, the last gasp of the Capricorn position, of the woman in control. The last degree of a sign could be seen as wise, although in a horary chart it would have no more power to influence events. The Moon's oppositions to natal Mercury and Pluto clearly feed into the difficulty we spoke of earlier in judging a situation. The Solar return emphasizes issues of perception.

Summing Up

Before we go into more depth about the Moon, I'd like to sum up what we've seen so far. First we looked at the solar return chart on its own. This is a particularly striking example, with so many planets angular. The group quickly grasped what issues might be described by Saturn, Pluto, Mars and Uranus angular: change and conflict, aggression and control, the need to defend her position against attack, the possibility for a radical shift in her professional life. These were all immediately clear. Imagine if they'd been Venus, Neptune and Moon on the same angles – the issues would be very different indeed.

Looking at the natal chart, we had more of a sense of how the birthday chart related to her deeper lifelong patterns, to her gifts and talents. Then, when we transposed the solar return planets around the birth chart, we added a layer; we saw close connections, degree areas, and particularly the importance of the financial axis. As I mentioned earlier, not all solar returns are alike. We all have quiet years, and we have quiet, uninteresting solar returns to go along with them. And some solar returns will look obscure, but come alive once you put them next to the birth chart. Aspects that repeat, or planets on significant degrees in the natal chart, or planets in the same houses, should all be given extra attention. They reveal degrees of connection and interrelated patterns that cannot be seen in the solar return alone. The angularity of the planets means the issue is likely to come to a crisis fairly early in the solar return year. Let me show you how this works. The year, for Martha, begins on the day of her solar return, August 3, 2001.

TIMING IN THE SOLAR RETURN

Using the Moon as a Timer

One of the simplest ways to measure time in the solar return is to move the Moon ahead by one degree a month. This technique has a correlation with secondary progressions, where one day equals a year in symbolic time. In the solar return the movement of planets in a twenty-four-hour period mirrors their symbolic movement during the year. Why one degree a month? The Moon averages about twelve degrees per day.

Audience: If the Moon is moving faster, say fourteen degrees a day, would you then adjust accordingly?

Lynn: Yes. If you want to be very precise, you would divide the Moon's diurnal movement by twelve, and progress it that amount each month. It can be a way of following events and aspects in the solar return, much as one would do with a horary chart. There are other methods of timing in the solar return, but this is the simplest and often the most revealing. In practice I find that moving each planet in the chart, not just the Moon, one degree per month, gives excellent results.

A Degree for a Month

Let's go back to Martha Stewart's solar return for 2001. The key events of the year occurred on December 27, 2001, when her broker, acting on a tip, sold her ImClone stocks, avoiding losses of $46,000. An FDA ruling meant the price dropped dramatically a few days later. If one degree of orb equals one month, we're looking for configurations in the solar chart with a four-degree orb. As it turns out, there are several factors at three and four-degree orbs, suggesting that November and December would be key months in the year. Let's list them:

- Saturn at 12°24' Gemini opposition Mars at 16°30' Sagittarius - Orb: 4° 06'
- Pluto at 12°39' Sagittarius conjunct Mars at 16°30' Sagittarius - Orb: 3° 51'
- Uranus at 23°20' Aquarius conjunct MC at 19° 55' Aquarius - Orb: 3° 25'
- Mercury at 7°57' Leo conjunct Sun at 10°57' Leo - Orb: 3° 00'

The SEC began investigating within days of the stock sales, and Stewart was quickly the object of intense media coverage. The solar return Moon was applying to both Neptune and Mercury seven months after her birthday, at a time when it became increasingly difficult to control her image. A key figure in the scandal was arrested in June 2002, and the stock in Stewart's company plummeted by over 5%. June is ten months after her birthday, and the solar return Moon opposed the Sun at that time, while the pressure continued unabated. The solar return Moon was at 29°52′ Capricorn, and the Sun was at 10°57′ Leo: an orb of 11°5′. Notice that none of these orbs gives absolute pinpoint precision. But they are close enough for comfort.[3]

Using the Sun as a Timer

Audience: I learned that the movement of the Sun through the houses of the solar return would be a good indicator for the major events of the year.

Lynn: This is a widely used technique in solar returns, and it often gives good results. In Stewart's case, the transiting Sun would have entered her solar 8th house on December 27 or 28, the date of the stock sale.

Audience: Talk about transgression, and other people's money! This sounds very exact.

Lynn: In June, when legal proceedings began to heat up, the Sun would have transited Saturn and then the Ascendant of the solar return, activating the original opposition. So again, this technique works particularly well in Stewart's example.

---

3   In 2004 she went to prison for five months.

UNDERSTANDING ASPECTS IN THE SOLAR RETURN

Aspects to the Luminaries

One of the things you will find is that aspects to the Luminaries become a major focus in the solar return. *Any exact aspect to the Sun is also a transit at the moment of the solar return.* If the Sun is square Saturn, we know that the transit is also taking place, so in some ways the solar return gives us a context for the transit. This is particularly important for outer planet transits which last for several years. The solar returns help us see if the transits will be felt internally or correspond to outer events; they give an extra layer of information. On the other hand, most of us will have a Jupiter-Sun conjunction in the solar return once every twelve years. We won't really interpret it all that differently from the Jupiter-Sun transit it is reflecting.

However, this is not necessarily true for aspects to the solar return Moon, which may have nothing to do with actual transits. In some ways, close aspects to the Moon turn out to be even more significant – you can't have a clearer indicator for the key issues in the year. These lunar aspects are strong even without an echo in the transits or secondary progressions. So I would suggest you pay close attention to them. You'll find that the solar return Moon's sign and aspects often describe the people we meet. I've seen many instances where the solar return Moon is in the sign of those who play a significant role during that year. Sometimes it's even within a degree or two of important planets in another person's chart. It can be quite uncanny.

Audience: I had always read that the Sun was the most important thing in the solar return, so I'm feeling slightly confused.

Lynn: Remember, the Sun is the basis for the whole chart. Because it is always in the same degree of the same sign, it doesn't really give us new information, but the Moon is different each year. The Moon becomes the principal mirror of its light, a pointer for the Sun. The Moon gives us the details, the rapidly changing events. When I look at the Sun in the solar return, there's always a feeling of familiarity. As psychological astrologers we are interested in how events touch the inner experience of the individual, and awaken or challenge the essential energies of a life, of a birth chart. And it is the Moon that points the way. At times the Moon seems to be the most important thing in these charts, but the chart is all about the Sun. I hope that's clearer.

Solar Return Moon Opposition Venus

Some years ago, in preparation for a talk, I researched a lifetime's worth of solar returns. As I ran through the charts, certain years stood out, and I'm going to show you one of these. The aspect patterns are spectacular – there's both a grand cross and a grand trine, and over the ninety years of this individual's life, there were only two other solar returns with a grand cross. You can see by the position of Pluto that this was a very long time ago; Pluto was in Cancer. Any comments?

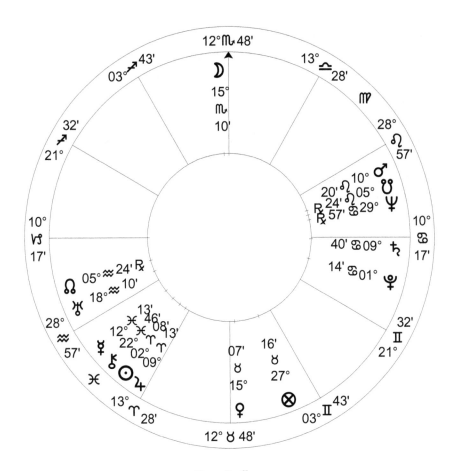

Dane Rudhyar
Solar return for 1916
Birth data: March 23, 1895, 12:42 am, Paris, France

Audience: There's a Moon-Venus opposition. Venus is very powerful, in her own sign Taurus, and on the IC. She even receives two sextiles to form a kite. She holds the center.

Lynn: How do you think that would work? The Moon in Scorpio is in fall.

Audience: If it were a woman's chart, I'd say there was a conflict between mother and daughter. Moon in Scorpio can be manipulative, primitive. Venus is in her own sign, which is relatively peaceful.

Lynn: I think that's beautifully expressed. Planets in solar returns can be acted out by other people; we draw them to us and invite them to be the actors in our play. This opposition is within minutes of exactitude: 15°07′ Taurus to 15°10′ Scorpio. It is at the heart of the year. The Moon in the 10th in Scorpio may very well represent the influence of a powerful woman, and this is the house of the mother. This is the solar return for a young man, aged twenty-one.

Audience: Saturn is opposite the Ascendant. With Saturn in Cancer, I wonder if this is about the need to break from the mother relationship. Perhaps he's met a woman and is in conflict between the two. Saturn rules the Capricorn Ascendant, so there would be a sense of responsibility. Is the choice between love and responsibility?

Audience: Could there be a child in the picture? The Moon is strong, but it's in detriment, and it's by itself high up in the chart. Is there emotional manipulation – a girl who gets pregnant, a relationship he doesn't want? Or, with Uranus opposition Mars, there could be a taboo, the wrong kind of relationship. It could be culturally or sexually inappropriate. Neptune is also in the 7th house. He isn't aware of what he's getting into.

Solar Return Jupiter Conjunct Sun

Audience: What about Jupiter? It's conjunct the Sun in Aries, so this should be expansive, confident, exciting. But Saturn seems to weigh him down, especially conjunct Pluto in the 6th. Someone is giving him a hard time - unless that points to a physical symptom.

Lynn: We're going to need to integrate the other planets in the grand cross. But if I sum up what's been said so far, the angular planets describe a situation where, in order to get what you want, you must separate from the past, say goodbye to something or someone you care about, and this will set up an emotional conflict. Saturn is on the Descendant, square the Sun: asking for a decision. It tells us that whatever decision he makes could affect his relationships for a long time. The impulse for a new beginning is very strong with Jupiter-Sun conjunct in Aries. Uranus opposition Mars is an aspect of risk, of daring, of surprise. He is an Aries, after all, and Jupiter conjunct Sun comes once every twelve years. It invites us to make our lives bigger, to begin a new phase of growth. Saturn on the 7th forming a square to Sun and Jupiter says there's a reason for caution, a barrier, or fear about going forward. Or perhaps there's simply a decision to make; we don't yet know which of these will win out. In the grand cross, the squares are between Moon-Venus and Uranus-Mars. Any ideas about that?

Audience: Emotionally it feels wild – trying to break with what's expected. Maybe it's a relationship that is broken off by someone else.

Audience: I have trouble seeing all those aspects together. Mars and Uranus square Moon might be unpredictable, angry. But I can't imagine that with Venus in Taurus. Venus is looking for harmony, isn't it?

Lynn: Imagine how difficult an aspect structure like this is for the person experiencing it! Usually one piece at a time is activated. We're pulled in one direction, then another, by the individual squares and oppositions. Sometimes it can feel as though we're being jerked around. Venus at the base of the chart seeks a solid ground for satisfaction, but square Uranus, it needs excitement and change. The square to Mars rushes into action, into desire. None of this is likely to flow easily into the Taurean need for stability. The squares to the Moon are particularly reactive, emotionally charged, high in color. Now, this would equally be the case if we were looking at individual squares, but the connection of four squares into a larger figure, the grand cross, brings something else into play.

A Solar Return Grand Cross

I have found that a grand cross in the solar return often represents a crossroads, a need to consciously choose a new path. Often there is a sense that destiny has given you a road map and a rather strong push in a particular direction. Sometimes there's a huge shock, but more often there's a sense that a path opens up and it's time to take it. The kind of choice will often depend on the planets and signs involved, but it may not always look particularly dramatic from the outside. Not everyone experiences traumatic events, and instead there can be a rather unpleasant feeling of being pulled in many different directions. It's not hard to imagine the endless internal conflicts pulling this way and that – not likely to be very enjoyable. Most people feel compelled to choose, and end up walking through one life into another. When that happens, the tension of the cross resolves itself through action. It may look ordinary from the outside – the decision to buy an apartment or to commit to a relationship – but it is rarely ordinary for the person involved. And looking back, there is often the sense that this year was the turning point, a year in which a whole new adventure began.

You may remember the eclipse in 1999, with a grand cross in Leo. So the Leos here presumably had grand crosses in their solar returns that year. Could you see it as a year of choice? You are smiling, Susan.

Audience: Every year is a year of choice!

Audience: I have the Sun in 20° Leo.

Lynn: So you would have been very connected to the eclipse. That was a key year for you. Did you feel that you were caught between choices?And did you make a major decision during that year? Yes?

Audience: I felt that everything was exploding around me. My job was a nightmare and I ended up leaving. I thought about separating from my husband as well, but we patched things together.

Lynn: Do you have the sense that you stepped through a kind of doorway?

Audience: Yes, I do. I experienced the grand cross in my solar return in the summer of 1999. It was so uncomfortable. I needed to make a decision to leave my job, but couldn't do it for many months. Things got worse and worse, until I finally made the leap. Listening to you speak about this brought the words "nailed to a cross" to mind.

Lynn: That kind of painful tension is something people often speak about with this kind of structure, but I find it more common when the grand cross is in fixed signs, or when Saturn puts the brakes on. Cardinal signs seem to spring into action much more quickly, and the same is true for mutable signs, to a lesser degree. Of course we need to take the planets into account. Let's go back to our example.

Audience: I wonder, with Uranus and Mars square Moon and Venus, does he run away from something he is afraid of? Or rush into something against his family's wishes? Jupiter-Sun makes me think of travel, of foreign countries.

Lynn: Yes, that's the key to the year. The year is 1916, in the middle of the First World War. Normally a twenty-one-year-old would have been in the trenches, with rather low chances for survival. The Saturn-Pluto conjunction is a collective aspect, and it marked a time when the world was in terrible upheaval. He was excluded from military service because of health problems. The regiment he would have belonged to was entirely wiped out. You'll notice he has Sun square Pluto almost exactly, so this is the year of the transit, a time which will change the way he sees himself forever. At that time, twenty-one was an age of maturity, of adulthood, in a very different sense than it is today. He was asking himself questions about his destiny, about what he was meant to do. He decided to embark on a great adventure (Jupiter-Sun), leaving his widowed mother behind. Perhaps he felt even more strongly called, having been spared by the war.

His great love was music, and thanks to his mother he'd been schooled in it very early, beginning piano at age seven. He was a composer of *avant garde* music, and had been invited to New York to perform one of his pieces. However, he didn't sail off alone; a woman was involved, a futurist painter, poet, singer and performance artist, who performed one of his compositions. Her name was Valentine de Saint-Point, and they sailed together with another young man in November 1916, eight months after his birthday. They had been invited to give a performance in New York. Notice the eight-degree orb between Mars and Uranus, and also between the Sun and Saturn. The transiting Sun would have gone over the solar return Midheaven and Moon at that time. Saint-Point had published a manifesto of lust, in which she wrote: "Lust is not, any more than pride, a mortal sin for the race that is strong. Lust, like pride, is a virtue that urges one on, a powerful source of energy."

Audience: She sounds like a good candidate for the solar return Moon in Scorpio!

Lynn: Indeed. It was a dangerous crossing, with submarine activity in the Atlantic, and certainly no easily booked return. The invitation turned out to be unsubstantial, though the concert did happen eventually. He never went back to France. Or rather, he went back as a visitor forty-two years later. What do we know about age twenty-one? What cycles are activated astrologically?

Audience: Saturn square Saturn, and Uranus square Uranus.

Lynn: That's right. It is often a year of choosing between tradition and individuation, between one's inheritance and an impulse to create an entirely new life. This is the solar return chart of Daniel Chennevière, the young Dane Rudhyar, who was to give birth to his new identity. He changed his name to Rudhyar, an interesting symbolic act which corresponds nicely to the Pluto-Sun transit. The following year he had a new Moon in the solar return.

Now, Rudhyar was an Aries with Moon in Aquarius, signs that are attracted to the new. We have a good idea which choice he's going to make! The solar return chart shows us the conflict, with Moon square Uranus, pulling to the future, and Saturn in Cancer on the Descendant the emotional hold of the past. Let's look at the natal chart with the solar return planets placed around it. Do you notice any connections to the natal chart?

A Natal Aspect Repeats: Moon Square Uranus

Audience: The solar return Moon is close to natal Uranus. And solar return Uranus is in the same sign as the natal Moon, not as close, but still conjunct. That seems very charged.

Lynn: These connections to the natal structure are extremely significant in the solar return. Once we see them, we know that the year is much more Uranian than we might first have imagined. The notion of change, of risk, becomes much stronger. In Rudhyar's case, the structure not only repeats but fits exactly on top of the natal pattern; the signs are reversed. It is the year of years, where Moon-Uranus releases its potential. On the solar return Midheaven, it takes direction of his life.

Rudhyar had a life-threatening operation when he was twelve, nearly thirteen, to remove a kidney and adrenal gland. I remember hearing Charles Harvey speak about his chart, and he pointed out how natal Mars in the 6th, conjuncts both Pluto and Neptune, and symbolizes this physical "sacrifice," a sacrifice that preserved him from death in the First World War. He stopped going to school, stopped playing the piano, and began to read a great deal. As a result, he finished his baccalaureate two years early, the same year his father died. His life became exceptional, and this must have reinforced a sense of increased free will, a notion of special destiny. Still, it was probably not easy to leave his widowed mother behind.

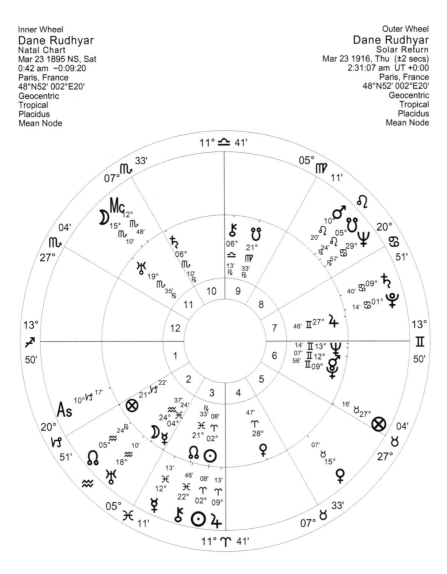

Inner Wheel
Dane Rudhyar
Natal Chart
Mar 23 1895 NS, Sat
0:42 am −0:09:20
Paris, France
48°N52' 002°E20'
Geocentric
Tropical
Placidus
Mean Node

Outer Wheel
Dane Rudhyar
Solar Return
Mar 23 1916, Thu (±2 secs)
2:31:07 am UT +0:00
Paris, France
48°N52' 002°E20'
Geocentric
Tropical
Placidus
Mean Node

Dane Rudhyar
Inner wheel: birth chart
Outer wheel: solar return for 1916

The Mars-Neptune-Pluto conjunction is angular and Mars disposits the Sun. Now, not everyone can handle a conjunction like that, but Rudhyar seemed to experience it as a wind gusting through him, a powerful impulse for creativity and for larger inspiration. He had a remarkable life. At the age of sixteen he met many extraordinary people, from Debussy to Eric Satie, and each of these meetings moved his life forward. He was in the audience when Stravinsky gave the first controversial performance of *The Rites of Spring*. He even worked briefly as a private secretary to the sculptor, Rodin. Later, in the United States, he met artists, dancers, composers, Theosophists and Zen masters. Rudhyar had Sagittarius rising and Jupiter in the 7th house. Although he went through periods of terrible poverty, he arrived in the United States at a time when it was rather common for wealthy patrons to offer help to struggling artists. Rudhyar would regularly be invited to come to a grand summer home for a season, to be given a place to live, or a stipend to write music. With Sun near the Aries point, he had an unstoppable creative energy, as a philosopher and a writer in addition to his real love, music. He was still composing music into his eighties, and he had a period as a serious painter. Perhaps it's the Uranus-Moon aspect that tells us he would be best known as an astrologer.

One thing you may have noticed is the absence of earth in Rudhyar's natal chart. He struggled financially most of his life, but with that strong Jupiter he also found patrons and benefactors. I want to talk about the Moon in the solar return, and then we'll come back to this theme.

CHAPTER TWO

THE MOON IN THE SOLAR RETURN

The Moon in the Elements

Of course we can never look at the Sun's light directly. It is easier to gaze at the soft reflected light of the Moon. In much the same way, each planet and its aspects in the solar chart reveals something of the solar year ahead. The Sun is the basis of the chart, so every planet is wearing solar colors, infused with the light of the Sun's return. We could do a delineation without saying much about the Sun, and it would still be present. The Sun, apart from its house position, is always the same, and so in an odd way it is a neutral point in these charts. Or look at it another way: it is so bright, so hot, so pure that we look instead to its changing relationships to the rest of the sky, and most particularly to the Moon. I would even say that the Moon is the key to understanding solar returns, although this at first seems contradictory.

One of the great gifts of astrology is the way it makes sense of our lives in terms of larger cycles, and the solar return is no exception. If we stretch our vision far enough, we see that we are looking at a larger, nineteen-year cycle that plays itself out in solar returns through the aspects between Sun and Moon. During this time we will experience almost every possible relationship between Sun and Moon: new Moons and full Moons, trines, sextiles, squares, as well as many minor aspects, and years without any aspect between the luminaries at all. Nineteen years later, the Moon will once again be very close to its natal position, and the cycle begins again.

I worked with solar returns very early on, and felt an immediate affinity with them. As people came back to see me over several years, I began to notice that the Moon would repeat in an element from one year to the next, and this held true for quite a number of charts. "That's odd," I thought. I started to run through the ephemeris and found that the Moon would spend two years, and often three, in the same element. It took quite a bit of time to confirm this kind of intuition before computers came along! My client work showed me that a process that begins when the Moon first enters an element often links these years together. And although solar returns were supposed to have an effect for one year and one year only, years with the Moon in a repeating element often have a connection. They come as a series, and things move on when the Moon changes elements. There was something empty about the usual way of looking at a solar return, grabbing at it hungrily, and tossing it aside after nine months. Solar returns are also part of the larger cycles in our lives.

Let me show you something that may help to make this clearer. This is a table with the Moon's position in a lifetime of solar returns – ninety years, to be exact. It's for Dane Rudhyar. If you look closely at this table, reading from the top of the first column down, you'll see that the Moon in the solar return moves through each element in the same order as they are found in the zodiac – fire to earth to air to water. The starting point depends on the element of the natal Moon, and from one year to the next the Moon will be either trine or quincunx by sign to its earlier position. Very rarely, the Moon will skip an element completely.

The Moon is so solicited by both the Sun and the earth's gravity that its orbit is irregular, so the Moon's measure is never quite the same from one year to the next. I've arranged the table in nineteen-year segments because each cycle lasts nineteen years, and then repeats with a few degrees of variation. I know, you're all saying, "What do we do with this?" It looks abstract, I know!

If you read the first column across, beginning with the natal Moon at 24° Aquarius you'll see that the Moon returns to this sign every nineteen years. Other columns will show a gradual shift across sign boundaries over time. The years in this first column, ages nineteen, thirty-eight, fifty-seven and seventy-six, are important years for those with strong Moon-Sun relationships, or who have an angular Moon in the birth chart. These are the years where the Sun and Moon find their original relationship. If we read down the second column, we can see the Moon's position in the elements from one year to the next. Let's begin with age twenty. As you see, there are two years with the Moon in water, three in fire, two in earth, and three in air. How do we work with these?

Dane Rudhyar Lifetime Solar Return Moon Placements

YR	Moon	YR	Moon	YR	Moon	YR	Moon	YR	Moon
0 A	24°37' Aqu (natal)	19 A	27°55' Aqu	38 A	27°20' Aqu	57 A	21°40' Aqu	76 A	14°49' Aqu
1 A	29°13 Gem	20 W	1°7' Can	39 W	6°24' Can	58 W	10°31' Can	77 W	9°21' Can
2 W	22°24' Sco	21 W	15°9' Sco	40 W	11°39' Sco	59 W	13°26' Sco	78 W	17°29' Sco
3 F	6°47' Ari New Moon	22 F	4°32' Ari New Moon	41 W	28° 48 Pis New Moon	60 W	24°8' Pis New Moon	79 W	23°6' Pis
4 F	13°47' Leo	23 F	17°53' Leo	42 F	18°1' Leo	61 F	12°51' Leo	80 F	5°28' Leo
5 F	19°50' Sag	24 F	20°4' Sag	43 F	25°31' Sag	62 E	0°11' Cap	81 E	0°24' Cap
6 E	13°17'Tau	25 E	6°21' Tau	44 E	2°15' Taur	63 E	3°13' Tau	82 E	7°7' Tau
7 E	27°4' Vir	26 E	25°5' Vir	45 E	19°25'Vir	64 Ear	14°19' Vir	83 E	13°28' Vir
8 A	3°25' Aqu	27 A	8°5' Aqu	46 A	9°21 Aqu	65 A	4°48' Aqu	84 E	27°7' Cap
9 A	10°49' Gem	28 A	10°26' Gem	47 A	14°49' Gem	66 A	19°45' Gem	85 A	21°9' Gem
10 W	3°57' Sco	29 A	27°20' Lib	48 A	23°1' Lib	67 A	23°17' Lib	86 A	26°45' Lib
11 W	17°18' Pis	30 W	15°26' Pis	49 W	9°42' Pis	68 W	4°11' Pis	87 W	3°02' Pis
12 W	22°36' Can	31 W	27°35' Can	50 W	29°53' Can	69 W	26°21' Can	88 W	18°27' Can
13 F	2°26' Sag	32 F	32 0°48 Sag	51 F	4°17 Sag	70 F	9°17' Sag	89 F	11°24' Sag
14 F	24° 27' Ari	33 F	18°21' Ari	52 F	13°44 Ari New Moon	71 F	13°38' Ari New Moon	90 F	16°34' Ari
15 E	7°39' Vir	34 E	6°26' Vir	53 E	0°36' Vir	72 F	24°34' Leo		
16 E	11°50'Cap	35 E	17°12 Cap	54 E	20°21 Cap	73 E	18°13' Cap		
17 E	23°29' Tau	36 E	20°22' Tau	55 E	23°29' Tau	74 E	28°16' Tau		
18 A	14°24' Lib	37 A	8°37' Lib Full Moon	56 A	3°54' Lib Full Moon	75 A	3°27' Lib Full Moon		

The Solar Return Moon in Air

In air, the solar return Moon pulls us out into contact with other people. It opens up the windows and doors, freshens our exchange with the world. The air signs rule the circulation of energy in the body, Gemini through the breath, Libra through the fluid balance, Aquarius through the circulation of blood; and each of these physical systems has a parallel in the world of relationships. New people breeze into our lives with the solar Moon in air, and sometimes new ideas sweep us along. Air Moon years almost always change the dynamics of relationship, the flow of contact and exchange, or they will reveal the difficulties we have in this area of life.

Moon in Gemini raises the curiosity quotient, pushes us to learn, to talk, to meet new people, and sometimes gets us back into a classroom. Communication becomes urgent. **Moon in Libra** brings a new awareness of our effect on others, on whether our actions create discord or harmony; it asks us to pay careful attention to partnership, but also to our inner balance. **Moon in Aquarius** may bring us into contact with a group or a community, but it can also bring out our quirky side. It encourages us to see things from the broadest possible perspective, and to enter into contact with systems, with objective models of the world. Our vision of life broadens and becomes less personal. All the air signs look for understanding and contact with others. These qualities are layered over our natal Moon – we are responding to them through our original filter.

Audience: I've brought my solar returns for the past few years, and I began coming to classes here with the solar return Moon in air. It's odd, because I'd really had my head down for the few years before that.

Lynn: I often hear things like that from groups – it seems to be fairly common. Then again, it's unlikely that it would be the only time someone would sign up for a class; there are other motivations for studying. Martha Stewart had been in a period of empire-building with the solar return Moon in earth, and it was at the last degree of Capricorn in 2001. The next two years she had the Moon in air signs. Air is the weakest element in her chart, and Stewart, in true Leo style, had built a business where she was at the center. During this two-year period she would have become acutely aware of the need for allies, counselors and supporters. She needed other people on her side. Although there may be a few hermits who function well without others, human beings are a profoundly social species. Air Moon years make us aware of whether we are well connected to others or not, of our system of relationship, and this isn't always comfortable.

The Solar Return Moon in Water

Beginning in 2004, her solar return Moon spends a three-year cycle in water. How would things change after the air cycle?

Audience: From extravert to introvert, I would think. This would be so much more personal. Water is intimate, it's more about feeling.

Lynn: Exactly. Air is famously detached, but when the solar return Moon enters water, all the ideas and experience of the air years move inward. They sweep through the cells of the body; they touch the level of feeling and soul. Water is deeply subjective, and deeply personal. It requires intimacy.

Audience: Doesn't water also have a universal side, as the great dissolver? Could it have to do with integrating thinking and feeling?

Lynn: Ah, that's very well put. This passage into water often corresponds to emotional and psychological integration. Ideas that had been purely abstract come in and become personal, but you're right to stress the larger dimension of water. The water element brings compassion and emotional understanding. These years can bring powerful emotional experiences. We ride the crest of feeling, and perhaps feel connected to others through the universality of human experience, the tenderness of love, or the sadness of loss. It can also correspond to a quieter period where closeness and sentiment are nourished, a time for family, or a desire for refuge. There is often a need for containment, for interiorization during the watery Moon years. One woman, who had successive solar return years marked by many water planets including the Moon, fell in love, and entered a deep lasting relationship for the first time, but also watched her mother die of cancer. Life can feel very full during the water Moon time. One thing to keep in mind is your relationship to each element in the birth chart. How comfortable are you with the watery realm? If you have many planets in these signs, it might feel familiar and agreeable, but the opposite could also hold true. Some people don't know how to swim, and are afraid of putting their head under water!

Audience: What about individual signs? Wouldn't Cancer be more connected to the need for refuge, and Scorpio more about passion?

Lynn: Yes, of course. Everything you know about the zodiac applies in solar returns, and brings nuance to each of the elements. Once the Moon enters an element, it moves in zodiacal order, but it may start with any of the three signs. With the **Moon in Pisces**, there is very little pretext of control. We're often overwhelmed by events that sweep through our lives, or are inspired and exalted by the muse. This is quite different from the protective feeling of the **Moon in Cancer**, the need to gather and enclose, or the driven, brooding intensity of the **Moon in Scorpio**. It is rare to sit on the fence with a Scorpio Moon in the solar return. Large undigested chunks of feeling will rise up, sometimes with great power, and can give rise to crises that allow for their release and elimination. But Scorpio can equally hold these processes inside, away from the view of the world. In Rudhyar's example, the Scorpio Moon was acting for natal Uranus, and square Uranus in the solar return. He plunged into life, into the unknown, without looking back.

The Solar Return Moon in Fire

After water, the Moon moves into fire, where the difference between elements comes with a particular impact. The boundary shift between these solar return years is usually noticeable, since we are moving from cold and wet to hot and dry. Symbolically, the shift from water to fire corresponds to the passage out of the womb into new life. There can be a sense of urgency as the vitality and life force of fire come through. What will these years be like?

Audience: Wouldn't there be passion and energy when the Moon is in a fire sign, more action?

Audience: It's extroverted again. I wonder if the fire doesn't dry up some of the feelings – no more clinging or hesitating. Fire can have almost too much energy.

Lynn: Yes, fire leaps out into life, it burns bright and gives warmth. Solar returns with the Moon in a fire sign often have an element of risk involved, impelled by an inner vision of what could be, what should be. One man I know, Victor, lost a well-paid, prestigious post in management with the solar return Moon in late Pisces. The Moon in Pisces often has a dissolving effect. When the solar Moon entered fire the following year, he made the decision to change careers, to use the transition to work more independently. He planned the business under solar return Moon in Leo opposition Uranus, and successfully made the career shift to consulting and training with solar return Moon conjunct Pluto in Sagittarius. The three-year fire cycle encouraged this adventurous approach to the future, and by the time the solar return Moon arrived in Aries he had an entirely new career.

Moon in Leo asks us to touch into our self-confidence, to open our hearts. **Moon in Sagittarius** connects us to our faith in a larger purpose, in the wide world, and **Moon in Aries** is the starting point for a whole new beginning. It helps us to find a way to act on our desires, even if it means fighting for what we want.

The Solar Return Moon in Earth

Audience: So the Moon in earth has to do with the world of money, with practical reality?

Lynn: That's certainly part of it. Earth knows how to build a foundation in the world, whether we're speaking of planting land, setting up houses, or building a business. It is at ease in the material. Earth loves productivity and accomplishment. It is also deeply sensual, practical, body-oriented. There's a focus on what works and what doesn't. Moon in earth can correspond to gardens and kitchens, to a hands-on creativity in dance or sculpting or ceramics that may have little to do with the bottom line. Delving into earth is necessary to replenish the spirit after a fire Moon time, to rebuild substance, to find stability again. We could spend much of the day talking about the elements, but there's too much to do, so I suggest you read Darby Costello's Element Series books.[4]

---

4   Darby Costello, *Water and Fire* and *Earth and Air*, Raven Dreams Press..

Now let's look again at the table of Moon positions for Rudhyar. He had no earth in his chart, so we'll take a closer look at what happens when he's in an earth cycle.

Audience: I know that people without earth are supposed to be ungrounded, but I have a friend like that who is financially very lucky. It's strange.

Lynn: I've observed something similar. It often seems that the absence of earth makes it easier to bend the rules of ordinary reality. For those with no earth, the fine print holds very little interest. Others watch them walk through life with an amazing lack of consciousness about real world issues.

Audience: My friends with no earth seem to be floating above their bodies. There's lots of inspiration, but not much practical awareness, and yet somehow they manage to function fairly well.

Lynn: In fact the earth Moon years in the solar return were times of great productivity for Rudhyar. In the first cycle at age seven, he began to play the piano. At age sixteen he published his first book, on Debussy. Again in 1922, with the solar return Moon in Taurus, he was commissioned to compose music for a play Pilgrimage *The Life of Christ* in Hollywood. These years seemed to usher in times when his many ideas were able to come into form. His compositions were performed, or his writing was published, or he earned a decent sum of money. In 1930/31, again with the solar return Moon in earth, he began to write astrological texts. Skipping ahead, to the ages of sixty-three, sixty-four and sixty-five, a series of solar returns with the Moon in earth signs brought a remarkable period of renewal. He returned to Europe, traveled, lectured, and began to publish his astrological writings in book form. Towards the end of his life, a remarkable four-year series of solar returns with Moon in earth began on his eighty-first birthday. On that birthday, a symposium was held in his honor. In 1976 and 1977, when he was eighty-one and eighty-two, he received grants from the National Endowment for the Arts, and in 1978 he received the Peabody Award. On his eighty-fifth birthday, the last year of this earth Moon cycle in the solar return, a concert was performed in his honor in New York. Quite extraordinary. In addition, a benefactor gave him a rent-free house to live in, so his material needs were taken care of during this time.

As an aside, when the Moon enters the Sun's element, it harmonizes with the Sun's basic intention, and a great deal can be accomplished. These can be years of harvest and attainment, of particular well-being, especially when the Moon and Sun are in trine. The conjunction between Sun and Moon can bring an important renewal, a new Moon in the solar return.

Aspects to the Solar Return Moon

Audience: I've been wondering about the interaction between elements and signs and the aspects the Moon makes – the outer planets especially. You mentioned Pluto in Sagittarius. It seems to me this will be quite different from the Moon in Sagittarius without Pluto – darker and heavier, less optimistic.

Lynn: Aspects are perhaps even more important than signs in the solar returns. You're right about Pluto's effect on the Moon. In Victor's case the career change was part of a larger metamorphosis. He was also changing in other ways, training in Chinese medicine, and turning into someone rather different from his old self. An outer planet bends and alters our experience of a sign for many years, and has a huge effect on any planet it contacts. This influence on the sign is part of the collective experience. It becomes very personal when it's mediated by the solar return Moon. Nevertheless, the sign and its element will still come through – in Sagittarius, his passion was channeled into a new philosophy of life, and he moved towards teaching and training, towards the role of the guide.

Fire has to do with joy and anger, but it spends what has been gathered in the watery Moon time; it releases strong feeling, it transforms and creates. There is a certain amount of risk. People are not hiding away when the Moon is in fire, and there can be a tendency to excess, to live with no thought for tomorrow. Fire can rage out of control, it knows no limits, so there can be a danger, too. There's a tendency to use large brush strokes, to step out into the world – the volume is turned up. This is particularly true for those who don't have a lot of fire in their charts to begin with; it tends to flip a switch.

Audience: Would that be true for other elements? For example, missing air or earth?

Lynn: Absolutely. Any emphasis in the solar return on something unusual or under-represented is worth keeping an eye on. It could mean an opportunity to wake up aspects of life that usually lie dormant, to acquire new experience, new skills. As the Moon moves around the zodiac in successive solar returns, we subtly shift our focus. It never replaces the natal Moon, but adds a sheen of sensitivity, of receptivity to other emotional perspectives in life. Those years where it lands in unknown territory are going to be particularly interesting. They give access to experiences that are usually unavailable, or land us in strange and unfamiliar places.

I can speak from my own experience. I do have some earth in my chart, but not very much. Years ago, when I moved to Paris, I was barely getting by, living in the country without working papers. I worked as a cook and struggled with French, doing readings when they came along. And although I had arrived saying,

"Money isn't important," I was getting mightily tired of having to count each *centime*. On my birthday, my apartment had been broken into, and the pitifully small amount of money I had was stolen. That was it. No more. I made a decision that if things didn't change I would leave. Then someone practically insisted I accept a job that gave me my *carte de sejour*. I had steadfastly refused to teach English, but this time I accepted, and it turned out to be extremely positive for me and invaluable for my work. I remember having the feeling of coming down to earth, of accepting the constraints of the real world. Later I realized that this inner decision was made when the solar return Moon went into earth signs.

Moon Opposite Uranus and Pluto on the Ascendant

Let me show you an example from many years ago. A student of astrology came to see me at the beginning of a solar year in which there were few major transits to the natal chart. Janice was forty-six at the time, divorced and living with her son. The solar return chart is striking for a number of reasons. First, Sun Mercury and Pluto are all conjunct the Ascendant, indicating a major change in perception and in identity. We spoke about the symbolism of birth and death associated with Pluto a little earlier today. But my attention was really drawn to the solar return Moon, because of its position as singleton in the 8th house, all by itself on the western side of the chart. At the time Chiron wasn't in general use, and I may not even have known it existed. What struck me was the emphasis on 8th house and Pluto themes, but even more, the exact-to-the-minute opposition aspect between Moon and Uranus. It seemed to jump out from the chart, demanding my attention. What kind of issues would come up with this?

Audience: In horary charts, an exact aspect has a fated quality. I'd wonder about inheritance issues with that aspect – something could suddenly change, through a shock or a death.

Audience: It feels exciting, but uncomfortable, too intense.

Audience: I was thinking about sex, myself! Couldn't this be an encounter with an absolutely irresistible Pluto type? A relationship that changes everything?

Lynn: I had that same feeling of intensity looking at the chart. Of course I also knew her a little, and was aware she lived in a fairly small apartment with her son. This configuration seemed to be insisting on change. I asked if she was intending to move or if there was any chance her son might go to live with his father. She was adamant that he was too young to go anywhere, just fourteen, and she was happy with her low rent living situation in a wonderful neighborhood. He was an angelic-looking blonde child with about six planets in Scorpio, whom she described as extremely sweet.

Audience: Uh-oh.

Lynn: Yes, that's what I thought. And I said she should probably be prepared for some kind of change. She was perplexed by the idea, since she had the ideal job, loved her neighborhood, and with natal Moon in Cancer she was extremely comfortable in the cozy duo with her son. Of course it made it impossible for her to have another relationship, but she didn't seem to mind.

Audience: Couldn't this be the solar return chart of someone who begins long-term therapy? Maybe it has more to do with a psychological breakthrough, or with delving into the unknown. The solar return Moon is in Gemini and, given what we've just said about the elements, there should be a desire to learn more, to understand things that hadn't been accessible until now.

Lynn: She was passionate about learning more about astrology, more about herself, and it was definitely a time of psychological awakening. The Moon in an air sign often brings a shift in relationship, and Gemini can bring us into contact with an *alter ego*, another aspect of ourselves, or the hidden side of a loved one. Many of the things that the group has suggested fit the events of this solar return, but not in the way you might imagine. About a month after her birthday, she found out that her son had been meeting a man in the park after school. He had even gone on a drive with this man, about forty kilometers outside of Paris, whom she described as dark and homely, a predator and a pedophile. Janice was terribly upset, and met the man, forbidding him to have any contact with her son. She sent her son to a therapist, and he seemed to understand the gravity of the situation. But then it happened again, and this time he had even allowed the man to photograph him, and he had posed naked for the camera. She found the photographs while cleaning out a desk. This is every parent's nightmare, that their child will be harmed or carried off; and this unsavory character certainly fit the description of a Pluto type. It's also a very graphic way to let your mother know your sexuality has woken up. Then, over the winter holidays, her son broke his leg skiing. They lived on the fifth floor without an elevator, so this kept him closer to home – for a while.

Audience: It sounds like her son was communicating something about his sexuality. And at the same time, he found a way to stop himself, to hold himself back.

Lynn: I think that's very accurate. She was so happy in her little bubble that she hadn't realized that she was too close to her son, that his sexuality had woken up, but even more, that he needed space in a way she didn't. Adolescents are almost psychic in the way they act out, touching into a parent's most hidden and vulnerable place, finding a way to break through their control. Not that any of it is conscious.

Audience: I keep thinking about the story of Persephone. There's such a strong Pluto theme here, with that Pluto rising in the solar return.

Lynn: That's true, and Janice is in the role of Demeter, keenly feeling the loss. When an aspect signature is particularly strong, it can correspond to these kinds of archetypal situations. Luckily she went into analysis and, especially after the second incident, came to the realization that her son was in urgent need of a man, and that she would reluctantly have to ask his father to intervene. This meant that, nine months after this solar return began, her son went to live with his father for the summer, and when the school year began he didn't come back. Although the exact Uranus-Moon aspect is really dominant, and the 8th house crisis reverberates all year, she was in an air Moon cycle. It did work in that way, pushing her out into contact with other people, and she became a serious student of astrology during this time.

Audience: That must have been very hard on her, to let him go when he was so young. I was noticing the Saturn-Venus conjunction in Scorpio in the solar return. That would also indicate separation, and mourning.

Lynn: It was very painful. Her divorce was extremely undigested, and the separation stirred up all those emotions. The exact Uranus-Moon aspect was extremely powerful. It literally blew apart her image of herself as a mother, and forced her to let go of her son. It also took the lid off her anger and resentment at her ex-husband.

Audience: Do you have any idea what was going on in her son's chart?

Lynn: Hold on to your hats! Her son, Jacques, was in the middle of a Pluto transit to his natal Sun at 3° Scorpio! Not only that, but his solar return Ascendant was at the very last degree of Libra, and conjunct both Pluto and Sun. That last degree tells us something is coming to an end; with the shift into Scorpio, it's a passage out of balance (pardon the pun) and into an extreme statement about oneself. There was no way he was going to remain a sweet little innocent, with those aspects.

Solar Return New Moon

A new Moon in the solar return always carries the energy of a new beginning. I'm sure none of you find that surprising! If the conjunction between Sun and Moon has not yet taken place, it is still technically a waning Moon, and we interpret things accordingly. With the Moon behind the Sun, a part of the solar return year will be concerned with finishing things, grappling with an old cycle. It is a time for clearing out, and a need to let go, a sense of being fed up with the old ways of doing things. Even while this is going on, an individual's attention will be on what is coming in; there will be an eagerness for movement, an anticipation of the new life to come.

Audience: What if the conjunction has already occurred – if the Moon is ahead of the Sun?

Lynn: In that case there's a good chance that something new has already begun by the time the birthday comes around. The year begins with a sense of freshness, and there's an open, optimistic approach to life. If something new comes up, we're likely to respond spontaneously, to say yes to what's being offered. There can be a quality of innocence to the new Moon – we are beginning again, discovering things for the first time. Of course a new Moon is in the same sign as the Sun, so we might think of it as self-renewal, as a new way of being with oneself. The Moon brings its vulnerability and sensitivity, its fecundating power.

Audience: What if the Moon has crossed over into the next sign? Is that still a new Moon?

Lynn: Yes, it still carries a freshness, a new Moon feeling, up to the semi-sextile, thirty degrees away. The Moon picks up the color of planets that are in aspect. Conjunctions are especially significant. These planets add their qualities to the picture. A new Moon in aspect to Saturn might mark the beginning of a long-term project, but it won't have the same ease or enthusiasm as one conjunct Jupiter.

Audience: The solar return lasts for twelve months. Is there some way of being more specific about timing, or of having an idea when to look for this renewal?

Lynn: If you use the Moon as a timer and move it one degree per month, it should give us an idea of when things will come together. The Sun and Moon will be in the same sign in the solar return at least once every nineteen years, usually more often than that. Given the symbolism of the new Moon, it's easy to see that these years would bring major new growth to an individual's life. There is often an entirely new person or place or experience that becomes the ground for the future. Aspects to the conjunction will give us an idea about how this might work out.

The Progressed Moon and the Solar Return Moon

Audience: This sounds a little bit like the progressed Moon to me. Is there a correlation?

Lynn: Not exactly. The Sun-Moon aspects in the solar return do not unfold in a logical, natural order through the houses and signs as they do in the progressed lunar cycle. They come and go at what seems an almost random rhythm, until we have taken note of the way the Moon cycles through the elements. And we're looking at a nineteen-year cycle in the solar return, while the progressed lunation cycle takes twenty-nine years.

Rudhyar's work on the progressed lunar cycle is one of the great contributions to astrology in the past century. There's an architectural feel to it, a scaffolding for an individual's development, and it gives access to a larger, long-term picture. I will always calculate progressions and use them side by side with the solar return. However, progressions other than the Moon change very slowly. One can work deeply with the sign and house of the progressed Moon, and many of you have followed Darby Costello's work on this. Solar returns are of a different nature. They are more like a close-up tool, a magnifying glass, that focuses attention in a quirky individual way, zooming in on this piece here, another totally different one there. I enjoy this work of going deeply into the moment, exploring it in detail. At the same time, I want to give you a sense that there is a larger process in the solar return. I hope this isn't confusing! Although it is probably best to use these as very distinct tools, there are moments when the two cycles come together. Usually a year or two before the progressed new Moon, you will find a new Moon in the solar return. It isn't always exact, but it's close.

New Moon Plenitude with Jupiter

A dear friend of mine, Jeff (chart follows), had a conjunction between Jupiter, Moon, and Sun in Taurus in his solar return for 1988. He had come to Paris looking for a new life, but was finding it a struggle financially. We joked about the Jupiter-Moon conjunction in the solar return chart and the lack of abundance in his life. And then he met a French woman and began a new romance. Within a few months she was pregnant. Their daughters are teenagers now, and the marriage has been a very happy one. The odd thing is that he had been married before, and tried to have children without success. He was fairly convinced he was sterile! So the notion of fertility with Jupiter-Moon was very literal.

Now, not every Jupiter-Moon conjunction will be accompanied by such spectacular life changes, although Jupiter-Moon will almost always give this sense that life is benign, that the universe supports your well-being and growth. I have seen it describe overly full emotional years, too, as if there's more amplitude to the feeling life. Perhaps it gives us mortals the ability to touch the emotions of the gods. In this case the energy of the new Moon brought Jupiter completely alive.

Audience: I have Jupiter-Moon conjunct in my solar return this year, but it doesn't feel anything like this. I've been all over the place emotionally.

Lynn: Sometimes Jupiter can externalize emotions; they may get bigger and bigger until they can't be contained. Emotions blow up to such a point that you have to laugh. Jupiter can exaggerate things so that they become absurd – you can't take it seriously any more. You know when you watch those horror movies where there are snails fifty-five storeys high. It can be that kind of change of perspective. You're terrified at first, overwhelmed, but then realize it's amusing.

Perhaps even more striking in Jeff's 1988 solar return chart is that strong Mars on the Midheaven. Mars helps us to act on our desires, to go out in the world and triumph. Here Jeff's triumph was personal rather than professional – he got the girl. Oddly enough, with Mars in Aquarius, they met in a group during a week-long residential workshop, and have stayed together ever since. Notice Mercury rising in Gemini, with Venus a bit further along in the 1st house, trine Mars and opposition Uranus in the 7th. The relationship began with music – a *bossa nova*. Things changed very quickly for both of them, and this is often the case with Venus in aspect to Uranus. This is the kind of solar return that typically corresponds to strong sexual or romantic energy, with both Venus and Mars close to the angles. In addition, the solar return Ascendant is two degrees away from natal Venus. This is a birthplace solar return, and it certainly fits the events we've been describing, even if he experienced them in a far away city on another continent.

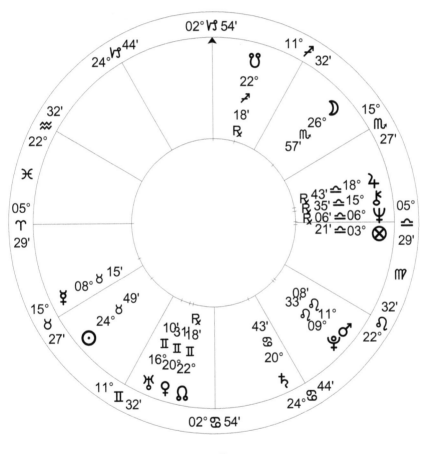

Jeff
Natal chart
May 16, 1946, 3:35 am EDT, New York, NY

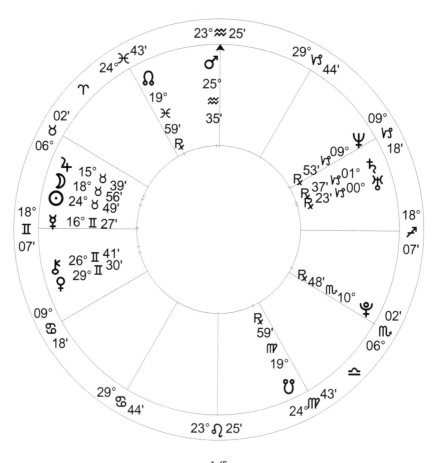

Jeff
Solar return for 1988, set for birth place

Audience: Gemini has an affinity to learning and teaching. I notice he's born with Venus conjunct Uranus, and they are in opposition in the solar return. That's another connection.

Lynn: Thanks for pointing that out; it also tells us that this is a man capable of falling in love very quickly. In many ways the structure of this solar return brings out the innate tendency to a whirlwind love affair, with the Ascendant of the solar return picking up the natal Venus-Uranus conjunction. There's also an exact conjunction between natal Uranus and solar return Mercury, and this gives a very fast pace to events, as well as a promise of unexpected events, a change in plans, a change in thinking.

New Moon in the Solar Return 12th house

Now, if we look at this chart set for the birthplace, the triple conjunction of Sun, Moon and Jupiter falls in the 12th house, and the 12th house has an odd way of bringing back issues from past cycles, for resolution or healing. This is particularly true when "easy" planets are found here. I always think of it as a place full of the unfinished or outgrown, the neglected or broken, but once a cycle of time has gone by, these undervalued pieces can be used again. It's like finding treasure in the attic. This was certainly Jeff's experience – he found something he'd been looking for. The 12th house is a harvest of the spirit; and despite the gloominess of most traditional texts on this subject, it can be a place of grace and resolution when favorable planets are found here. It can also carry a fated feeling, a locked-in, haunted sensation. With difficult planets like Saturn or Pluto, it can feel as if the fates are breathing down your back, hounding your every move. Even then, if you do the work, they won't necessarily be problematic. Planets in the solar return 12th are asking to be assimilated, and then they release their power.

Audience: But the love story began during this solar return, with planets in angular houses. It doesn't sound 12th house to me.

Lynn: Ah, that's true, but there was a whole new life to come, preparing itself in that 12th house. Many romances come and go. Here the 12th house has the sense of gestation, and in this case it was quite literal. The woman he met and fell in love with is strongly Piscean, which may be another way to think about all those planets in the 12th house. This new relationship, with its promise of a fertile future, is partly symbolized by the conjunction of Jupiter, Moon and Sun. They stayed in France until their daughter was born, and moved to the United States a few months later, in his next solar return. So this 12th house year can be seen as a period of transition. His progressed new Moon was about a year after the move. I mention this because, if you begin working with solar returns, you'll notice there's often a solar return with a new Moon phase just before or after the progressed new Moon. It will give you a clue as to when the new energy begins to bubble up in a person's life.

One more thing: Jupiter is in his natal 7th house, and so in his case it has an affinity for relationship. Jeff's wife came from a warm, close, loving family. He found himself part of this extended French tribe, lovers of good food and wine, open and unfazed about sexuality, a Taurus dream come true. This brought another dimension of healing, since his own family of origin was disconnected and unemotional. I asked him what words he would use to describe the abundance of this solar return year, since it certainly wasn't about money. He said, "Love, sex, food, wine and babies."

Remember the nineteen-year cycle I mentioned? Jeff also had a new Moon in the solar return nineteen years earlier, in 1969, the year he got out of the navy. He initially went back to live with his family, and was quite active in anti-war events. He also drifted into studying various metaphysical subjects, which would much later lead to a new career. That new Moon was in the 8th house, opposition Neptune, and it began with an affirmation of values: an ex-military man standing up against the war, as well as a strong divergence with his father over what was important in life. It probably had more to do with undoing, than doing - a state of things rather commonly associated with Neptune.

Audience: I find it interesting that the Nodal cycle is about the same, nineteen years. Would there be a correlation with the Saros cycle as well?

Lynn: All of these are different ways of looking at the alignment between Sun, Moon and Earth over time. The Nodal cycle is actually a bit less, 18.6 years, but it is certainly in the same ballpark. And you will see that an eclipse in a solar return will repeat nineteen years later. I imagine that, over a lifetime, it could be interesting to see which Saros cycles weave into our solar returns. They might very well describe a key theme playing itself out in an individual's life. Bernadette Brady would be the person to speak to about this.

Solar Return Full Moon

Audience: What happens when there's a full Moon in the Solar return? Would it be a positive indicator?

Lynn: How do most of us experience the full Moon each month? Sometimes it is charged and overwrought, at others there is a sense that all is right with the world.

Audience: It could be as good as it gets, a time of reaping rewards.

Audience: Fruition. That's the sort of word Rudhyar would use.

Audience: Something could be polarized, pushed to an extreme.

Lynn: Full Moon years are rarely calm. They can be years of major crises that bring us face to face with the great questions in life, or they can be years of wonder and excitement, of peak experience and rare insight. Planets in aspect to the Sun and Moon, particularly conjunctions and squares, will have a powerful effect, beaming through the lens of the Sun-Moon opposition. One particular house axis will be strongly lit up by the Sun and Moon, and the effects of the opposition will be especially felt in the areas of life symbolized by these houses. In the 1st and 7th, the full Moon can push relationship issues to a climax; there may be a crisis or a separation, but it could equally symbolize the fullness of love. One man had decided to leave his partner only to learn she was pregnant. He spent much of the solar return in a state of conflict about whether to stay or go. When the child was born, he entered into a relationship without ambivalence for the first time. Through the events symbolized by the full Moon, we become conscious of how we are tied to others, and how much they mean to us. This doesn't happen exclusively in partnerships or marriages. It can touch any relationship where the experience of the other has a particular fullness, a particular quality of acknowledgement.

Audience: I'm wondering whether the same kinds of conflicts and changes would be true of other oppositions, and not only the full Moon?

Lynn: That's a good question. The oppositions between houses have an archetypal signature, and this is always activated with planets in opposition, so the essence of what I'm saying can be used in interpreting any two planets in opposition. You'll need to factor in the nature of the planets. What makes the full Moon unique is its ability to bring light to darkness, its possibility for enlightenment, for a breakthrough in understanding.

A Solar Return with an Eclipsed Full Moon

Let's look at another of Rudhyar's solar returns, a year with a full Moon, and an eclipse, at that. In 1932, he was thirty-seven years old. By this time a terrible economic depression had dried up support for the arts. Rudhyar had met Marc Edmund Jones, and began to be interested in Jung. An earlier interest in astrology suddenly came together with a much larger philosophical and psychological framework. The full Moon falls across the 4th/10th axis. This year marked a decisive shift for Rudhyar, when he began writing for a new astrology magazine created by Paul Clancy. When it failed, another magazine began the following year, and Rudhyar's career as an astrological writer was launched. As time went on, he wrote several articles each month for *American Astrology*. So how to understand this Sun-Moon opposition?

Audience: The Sun is in the 4th house. He found a new base, and with Moon in the 10th, a new public.

Audience: The eclipse must indicate a major change; a shadow passes over the Moon.

Lynn: You're right. This was a time when Rudhyar's musical career was blocked. He was also in rather poor health. Writing wasn't new for Rudhyar, but writing became the major focus of his creativity for many years to come. And this is reinforced by a Mercury-Uranus conjunction square Pluto. This was a time of major new insights, an integration of ideas, and a new depth and purpose. It was the beginning of a whole new career, and a breakthrough in his understanding. Moon and Sun are sextile and trine a 2nd house Saturn, and Rudhyar began to earn his living through astrological writing rather than composing.

Audience: So the opposition brought a career crisis. I wonder if he was depressed, and that had something to do with the health issues.

Lynn: You may well be right. With the full Moon in the solar return, some sort of inner conflict or polarization will be brought to an extreme. It is likely to be acted out within the area of life symbolized by the houses. Here, the 10th house is the house of career.

This year was both difficult and wonderful. There can be a trade-off in any opposition, where one path becomes blocked while another opens. The eclipse is a moment of particular alignment; it occurs with the Moon and Sun on the ecliptic, where planets pass from north to south latitude. So it also carries this notion of change in direction. For Rudhyar, it brought a new understanding of astrological ideas, and the power of this insight opened up a whole new career as an astrological writer. Moon in the solar return 10th house brought a change in direction.

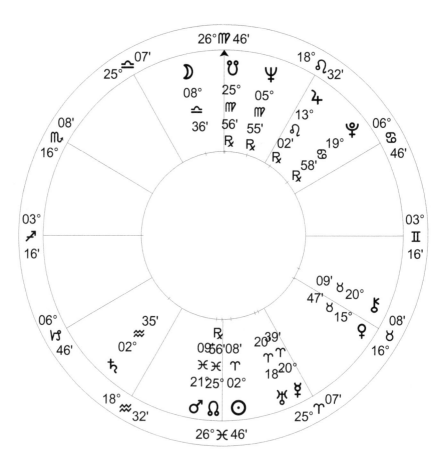

Dane Rudhyar
Solar return for 1932, set for birthplace

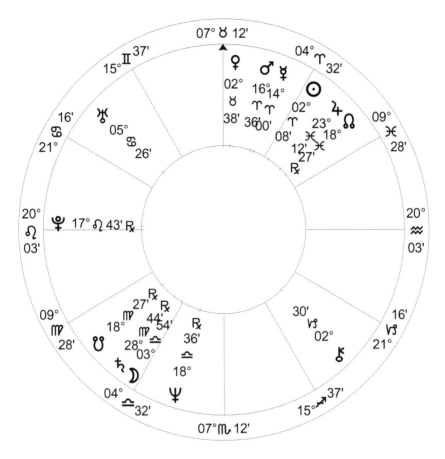

Dane Rudhyar
Solar return for 1951, set for birthplace

Audience: You could call that opposition a shock corridor that you have to walk down.

Audience: The choice is so clear. In order to come home – Sun in the 4th – you have to get off the fence. You can't be in both places at once. It seems to me that the full Moon period brings a contradiction, which you probably don't realize is there until it suddenly pops up and says, "Here I am."

Audience: Both Pluto and Jupiter are in the 8th. Something ends financially, too, but a new opportunity arises. The 8th connects to psychology, so he is asked to grow there.

Audience: So an opposition across the 4th/10th axis of the solar chart brings a professional crisis?

Lynn: That's certainly a possibility. Once again, we're looking for the dynamics that underlie events. I could give you an endless list of facts about each house, most of them already familiar, but that may not be very helpful. The conflict set up between these houses is often one where security needs do battle with our drive for accomplishment, for success. It can be as simple as not having enough hours in the day to give adequate time to both work and family. Or it can reveal a major conflict between inner needs and outer commitments, one's private life and professional imperatives. The full Moon here may make us very aware of our family inheritance, of a possible battle between the maternal and paternal side in our ancestry and their effect on our life direction. We feel simultaneous pulls from the past, from family, and our desire to step into our calling in life. Oppositions can also be experienced as a strong flow of energy between planets, especially when they come with awareness; and if all goes well, a great deal can be built and established with the full Moon here.

Nineteen Years Later: Full Moon Again

Since you're now all aware that the solar return Moon returns to the same area nineteen years later, you won't be surprised to find another full Moon in Rudhyar's solar return for 1951. Let's have a look. This time the Sun-Moon opposition falls across the 2nd and 8th houses.

Audience: Saturn is conjunct the Moon in the 2nd house. That can't be good for his finances.

Audience: But Jupiter is in the 8th opposing Saturn, so that might help. Is there a transfer of wealth?

Lynn: In a manner of speaking. There was indeed a financial crisis. *American Astrology*, which had been the mainstay of Rudhyar's writing, stopped publishing, and his income dried up. Notice the strong connection between events in these two solar returns, nineteen years apart. What began in one ended in the other. Perhaps this is a function of the eclipse, but it's certainly worth thinking about solar returns with important aspects between the Sun and Moon. There may be a connection to the earlier cycle. Rudyhar's young wife, Eya, the second Mrs. Rudhyar, had trained with Joseph Moreno, the founder of psychodrama. He'd recommended she be chosen to create and direct a department of psychodrama at an institute in Iowa. The focus shifted to Eya, and she became the breadwinner. Rudhyar felt stranded in the middle of the cornfields, with little outlet for his creative interests. He wasn't able to find a publisher for his work during this time.

Audience: Venus is on the Midheaven and Pluto is rising. That describes a powerful woman.

Lynn: I believe she was powerful, and beloved. She was a dancer and a psychotherapist, and Rudhyar was enchanted with her, very much in love. Unfortunately, this time in Iowa turned out to be traumatic. Eya eventually had an affair with one of her students and asked Rudhyar for a divorce a few years later. We could see this chart as a shift in the power balance of the relationship. Pluto rising reinforces the Sun in the 8th house. The eclipse is very wide, but still in effect; he went into a period of occultation.

Audience: Uranus was also square the Sun. I would have expected change and excitement.

Lynn: It was a huge change. They were far from New York, and far from New Mexico, where they were very much part of the artistic and spiritual scene. The Uranus transit was slightly past (exact). But I would agree – the atmosphere of this time feels more Plutonian than Uranian. Uranus destabilized things, and he experienced a loss of power. Leo is intercepted in the 8th house in Rudhyar's natal chart, and it comes out on the Ascendant in this solar return. All these factors point to an ego death, and a transformation to come. At the same time, secondary progressed Mercury had come up to conjunct Mars and Neptune in the birth chart.

Audience: And Mercury rules his 7th house of relationship.

Audience: You haven't got the solar return for when he met Leyla, have you? That is an interesting story.

Lynn: I do have that chart. It was in 1974, when he was seventy-nine years old and she was in her twenties. She became his collaborator and co-author, and did a great deal to promote his music.[5] The rulers of the solar return 1st and 7th houses, Mercury and Jupiter, were conjunct in the 1st house that year, and it was an almost new Moon. Rudhyar really did have an exceptional life. He had a third wife before he met Leyla, also a much younger woman, named Tana. The Jupiter-Mercury conjunction also showed up in the solar returns for the year he met Tana and those when he met his other wives as well. He certainly lived out the diversity and multiple promises of a natal 7th house Jupiter in Gemini.

---

5   See the Appendix.

Solar Return Full Moons in Other Houses

The full Moon in the **2nd and 8th houses** of the solar return chart often stirs the hornet's nest of jealousy or passion, possessiveness or power. And it deepens our understanding of psychological patterns of intimacy and sexuality. It can bring an important change in the way we handle money; there can be reversals, or a major financial breakthrough. Again, the aspects will give us clues to the finer workings of the opposition. You are all aware of the usual associations of the 8th house to death, sex and taxes. Events in these areas come and test our solidity, our ability to hold onto what matters to us, or ask us to accept an end and move on with our lives. They invite us to delve more deeply into our own unconscious.

In the **3rd and 9th houses**, there can be a complete change in our thinking, or a situation of constant and exhausting disagreement. The full Moon here could signal a major discovery, a sudden experience of insight or illumination. But it could also bring considerable stress, a sense of being pulled back and forth between the conscious and unconscious mind. Since this axis has to do with journeys, it can intensify any experience of traveling, with possible dramatic experiences lurking around a bend in the road. One young woman began a full Moon solar return chart with a wrenching disagreement. The conflict bubbled away for months, leading to a short period of depression, followed by illuminating dreams that helped her see things from a much larger perspective. She traveled far from home for the first time. In the end she had a peak year in her university studies, winning a special award, but there was another crisis of meaning. She was struggling to find the reasons behind her experience, and it led to an intense interest in philosophy and metaphysics.

A solar return full Moon across the **5th and 11th houses** can set in place a tension between the pleasures of the moment and our long-term goals, our hopes for the future. It also asks us to look at how we are connected to others, to the community, to a vision of the world. How do the very personal choices we make with lovers or children affect the world as a whole? Are we caught in group-think and unable to follow our heart, our creative path? One woman with a full Moon here emigrated and found herself in a much more restrained culture; she constantly felt too loud, too bright, too exotic, as if other people disapproved of her slightly. She had to learn a new way of relating in order to find her place. The full Moon here will illuminate our sense of what we do to get love and attention, and how living our ideal –or not – touches the lives of others.

We've spoken about the 12th house and its promise of healing. When the **6th and 12th houses** are involved by opposition, there is often a breakdown in the body or the emotions, the need for a physical or psychological crisis to break out of limiting patterns. It can also bring a peak in the expression of long-developed skills, as it did for Muhammed Ali in 1965, the year he won the World Championship for the first time. For others, the soul can be caught in the daily grind, worn down by a sense of bondage, a lack of choice, all too often reflected in the way we experience work, or the necessary tasks of daily life. A solar return full Moon across this house axis makes us aware there's more to life than this, and we can step out of the ordinary into truly altered states of consciousness. The full Mystical Monty is a possibility.

CHAPTER THREE

LOCATION, LOCATION, LOCATION

There is a great deal of agitation around the question of location in solar returns. Should we relocate to the place of residence? Calculate for the place we happen to be on the day of the solar return, or use the place of birth, as we do for progressions? I have gone back and forth over this question in my work with clients, and have found that it's a mistake to overlook the solar return for the birthplace. When planets are angular in the birthplace solar return, they will be extremely active during the year, and you ignore them at your peril! It's been an important question for me since many of the people I work with come from abroad, or were born in other regions of France. And I live in France, one fourth of the globe away from my birthplace. Most of the work I will present today uses the place of birth. This said, I have found that relocated charts often carry similar themes, but shown from another perspective. Not long ago, I was teaching a seminar at Karen Hamaker-Zondag's school in Amsterdam; she is an advocate of relocation, but both of us were surprised at how the charts seemed to work together, as if we were adding layers of meaning. She suggested that the birthplace solar return indicated a potential and that the relocated chart was a place of action. We could compare it to the right and left hands in palmistry, where the hand you use most reflects the way you have developed your potential.

Earlier, when we looked at Jeff's example, I was using the chart set for the birthplace, in New York City. The Ascendant degree is conjunct his natal Venus-Uranus conjunction, a particularly strong indicator for an important love story, as well as Mars and Venus close to the angles. If we relocate the chart for Paris, the Jupiter-Moon conjunction comes onto the MC, and Mars is on the Descendant. These are also strong placements, but there's much less of a Venus signature to things.

Audience: Could the two charts be working together? After all, Jupiter-Moon on the MC makes sense for the story of the child.

Lynn: It's highly likely there's a dialogue between the two. I think that when you are simply working with your own chart or those of close friends and family, you can keep adding variables; but in client work this is harder to do. You need to make a choice at some point.

Audience: I was born in the Middle East, but I left as a child. I always thought I should calculate the solar return for the place I live. That makes more sense to me.

Lynn: Yes, I can understand that. Calculating the chart for the place of residence also makes more sense to me than dashing off to a faraway place in order to have the "best" solar return. This is one of the most controversial areas in solar returns. I know that many astrologers advocate this approach. To me this is as much a question of philosophy as it is of practice. I have known people who flew to Martinique so that they could escape a Saturn-Mars conjunction on the solar return Ascendant. As a magical act, as a therapeutic gesture, this makes sense to me. It's a way of dealing with possible anxiety about difficult aspects, and you can work on your suntan at the same time! As we know, a little knowledge is a dangerous thing, and despite all our attempts to assuage anxiety about "bad" aspects, relocating oneself for the solar return is one way to feel you're taking things into your own hands.

Audience: I know someone who would fly all over the world, even for just one day. I think he always wanted the Sun in the 2nd house. As a result of doing this, he was earning so much money he could afford to keep doing it.

Lynn: I think we could argue about what is cause and what is effect. Does fate really work that way? I often think about what the Balinese say when there's an accident with a westerner. It doesn't matter who ran into whom. For them the accident is clearly the westerner's fault, because they don't belong there in the first place. Certainly, as astrologers, we all believe in working with the planetary energies, rather than going against them.

Alexander Volguine, who wrote the classic French text on solar returns, openly wrote about the practice of relocating a chart as astrological magic. Electional charts are similar. They are a way of gathering our intention for an upcoming event. I would still suggest you look at the solar return for the place of birth – just put it up and observe. And then there's the famous story of the man who catches a glimpse of Death in the streets of Isafahan. Death turns and looks at him in surprise. The man is struck by a wave of terror, jumps on his horse and rides like a fury to Samarkand. He goes to an inn and collapses in exhaustion. At midnight he hears a knock on the door. Death is standing there, saying, "I'm glad I found you. I couldn't conceal my surprise this morning in the market at Isfahan, because I knew we had an appointment here in Samarkand tonight."

Audience: That's from a Somerset Maugham novel.

Lynn: I believe he adapted it from a Sufi teaching story. The question remains: How much can we change by traveling to another place for our solar return? The degrees of the planets, their aspects and signs, will not change, but the houses will. Some very respected people say that all of astrology is a magical act, that it isn't so much about truth as about divination. Other astrologers suggest shifting the house angles as you move from one place to the next. I once had a solar return with rather difficult planets on the angles. I took a three-month sabbatical traveling in Asia, and that time had a very different feel to it than the rest of the year; but I'm not sure I would attribute this solely to the changing solar return. I would suggest putting the solar return charts for the place of residence and the birth place side by side. Do your own research.

RELOCATED SOLAR RETURNS

Steven Spielberg

Let's look at an example. Steven Spielberg was born December 18, 1946 at 6:16 pm in Cincinnati, Ohio. As you can see from his natal chart, he has a very strong 5th house, with an imaginative Moon, Venus, Jupiter and Chiron all placed in Scorpio. I've always been struck by his ability to create exciting, amusing films about genuinely scary things, often from a child's point of view. This fits with his Cancer ascendant and its ruler, the Moon, in the 5th house. A Pisces Midheaven is common in the charts of artists, dreamers and visionaries – right at home in Hollywood. *Duel*, his first film, is about a faceless truck driver looming relentlessly from behind, trying to run a car off the road. *Jaws*, with its terrifying music, taps into the age-old fear of what's hiding in the deep, and *ET* gives us the unknown from a child's perspective, presenting a choice between wonder and love, fear and destruction. Even the most cartoonish of the early films, *Raiders of the Lost Ark*, has scenes of serpents, spiders and death-heads, all laughed away by Jupiter and a strong Sagittarian spirit. In December 1993, when *Schindler's List* was released, Spielberg was the most successful director of all time in terms of box-office, but there was still a question about whether he could make a serious film. It's fascinating to see that his Moon is square Saturn and Pluto, hardly a lightweight aspect. His films had won many awards, but he'd never been tapped for Best Director.

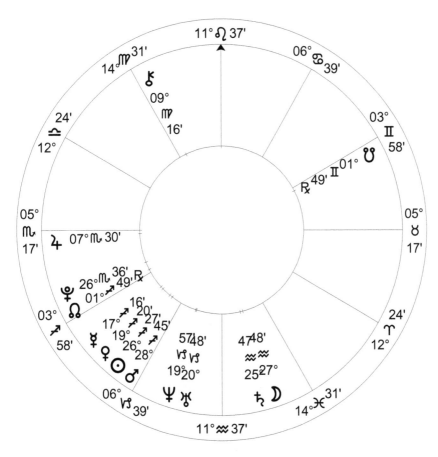

Steven Spielberg
Solar return for 1993, set for birthplace

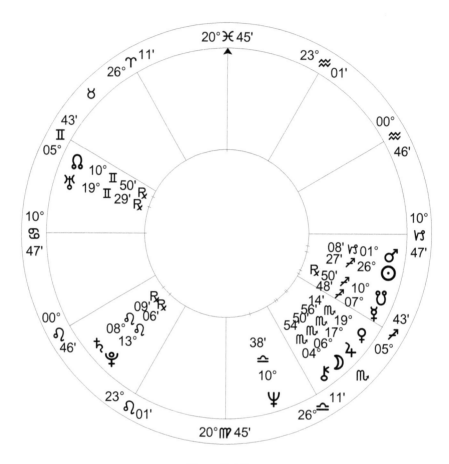

Steven Spielberg
Natal chart
December 18, 1946, 6:16 pm EST, Cincinnati, Ohio

Degree Areas in the Solar Return

Let's look at his 1993 solar return for Cincinnati, his place of birth. Jupiter immediately leaps to our attention - at 7° Scorpio, it conjuncts the Ascendant at 5°. This is already promising enough, and gives a clear indication of personal success. But even more, Jupiter is within one degree of the natal Moon, as is the Ascendant. No matter where he lived, or where he found himself at the moment of his birthday, 1993 would be a year where Spielberg's natal Moon would be in full flower.

Audience: Would the connection to the natal Moon's degree be similar to a conjunction?

Lynn: Something like that. Whenever a planet in the solar return is on or near the degree of a natal planet, we can say that it is acting *for* that planet this year. It becomes the transmitter for the natal planet. In this case Jupiter had just transited Spielberg's natal Moon, a period of heightened, usually positive feeling. The film had been released to mostly rave reviews just two weeks before, on December 1, 1993.

Audience: The Ascendant falls in the 5th house of the natal chart, and he has Moon, Venus and Jupiter there. Great for creativity, for popularity.

Lynn: And the 5th house is the house of our creative children. This solar return speaks to the film's "birth" in the world; the writing and filming and planning had all been done in the years before. If we continue the metaphor, Jupiter on the natal Moon's degree brings a successful birth, a happy outcome.

Audience: It seems there's a contradiction here, since the solar return Moon is conjunct Saturn. I wouldn't know how to judge this combination. Which is stronger?

Lynn: We would have to conclude that they're working together. You might say that this was Spielberg's first grown-up film. It was a black and white film on a difficult subject, one that is usually box office poison. A dignified Saturn with the Moon in Spielberg's solar return 4th house certainly describes deeply felt, yet uncomfortable emotions. And these feelings are also part of his cultural and familial inheritance. In *Schindler's List,* he is speaking for a whole community. With Moon and Saturn in Aquarius, he is connected to something larger than himself, in a personal, 4th house way.

Audience: What about the cycle of elements for the solar return Moon? Natally he has a watery Moon in a sign of strong feeling – Scorpio. How does the air of Aquarius affect that?

Lynn: Thanks for your question. Air gives objectivity to water. It brings distance and perspective to something very personal. I wonder if it would have been possible for Spielberg to make this film without the strong air Moon. This is the second year of the Moon in the air element. Let me tell you its aspect structure for the 1992 solar return, so you can see the connection between the two years: The Moon was conjunct Jupiter in Libra with both of them trine a conjunction of Venus and Saturn in Aquarius.

Audience: Wow! It's so similar to the year we've been looking at – with both Jupiter and Saturn in aspect to the Moon by trine. It looks like a great solar return for working with other people.

Lynn: Yes, exactly, the years are strongly connected. This is why I started paying attention to the Moon cycle in the solar return. I was seeing these kinds of links far too often for it to be over-looked. By the way, that 1992 Jupiter-Moon conjunction was close to natal Neptune, and trine to natal Uranus. The solar return planets intensified a natal aspect and filled in the third trine, making a grand trine when we superimpose the two charts. In his treatment of the Holocaust, Spielberg chose to focus on the importance of kindness, of altruism and common humanity, in one person's story. Schindler was no saint; he begins as a rather self-centered businessman essentially motivated by money and self-preservation, but he becomes almost exalted by the desire to help, to undo harm.

Audience: From what you're saying, the combination of Scorpio and Aquarius in the 1993 solar return helped him touch people by showing deep, almost unbearable feelings with restraint. Perhaps those feelings were contained by an intelligent Saturn?

Lynn: What a wonderful way to sum it up. Look, there's more. Do you see another natal degree area picked up by the solar return?

Audience: It's Pluto! Or rather, Saturn-Pluto – the Midheaven at 11° Leo picks up the natal Saturn-Pluto conjunction at 8° and 13°. I have been thinking that Pluto should be here somewhere – it is a film about the Holocaust, after all.

Lynn: Aren't these connections to the birth chart fascinating? The degrees of Saturn and Pluto on the solar return Midheaven brings this natal conjunction out to the world, and this is the year Spielberg was recognised for his ability to treat the dark side, to show what he really felt, to touch the horror of what the Jewish people went through in the Second World War. At the time, people walked out of the film stunned, immensely moved. The Midheaven is about bringing things up to the light. We might wonder if Spielberg had not always held back his deeper feelings under a congenial and optimistic Sagittarian surface. This was the year all that changed, as far as the outer world was concerned. Can you see that the birthplace solar return acts as a template of sorts? Now, not every year will have this kind of structure, but when you find it, something fundamental is emerging.

By the way, age forty-seven also corresponds to a Mars return. It's often an important year for those with Mars strong in the natal chart. As for Pluto, it is square the Moon-Saturn conjunction, and certainly present in this solar return. It was angular for the birthplace in the previous solar return for 1992, during the making of the film – on the IC, in fact, tapping into a deep source, bringing up a powerful, unsettling stream of memory. It must have shaken a great deal inside him to deal with the subject. These kinds of mysterious links from one solar return to the next are not uncommon, when you do solar returns for the birthplace.

Spielberg's Relocated Solar Return

Now, what do we find in the relocated chart? I am assuming that Spielberg spent his birthday in Los Angeles, where he has his home.

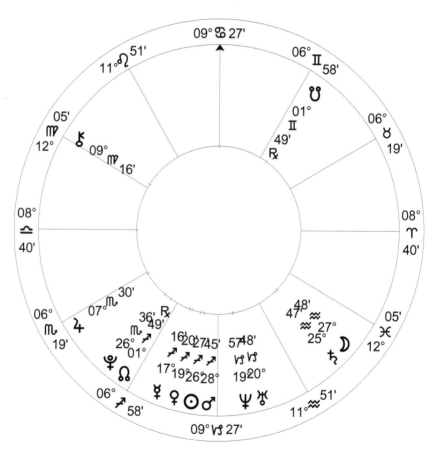

Steven Spielberg
Solar return for 1993, relocated to Los Angeles, California

Although no planets are angular, Jupiter is in the 2nd house trine the Midheaven. Since the 2nd house has to do with talent, this would be an extremely favorable indicator for recognition. Earth houses are often literal; they bring tangible rewards, things you can take home and put on a shelf. The Midheaven degree is close to the natal Ascendant, and the relocated solar return Ascendant is on the degree of natal Neptune: something dreamed of can come into being this year. The Ascendant-Neptune connection also brings up issues of sacrifice and redemption.

This is certainly one of the subjects of *Schindler's List*. Spielberg had been planning a film on the Holocaust for ten years, and this chart, with the connection between the 2nd and 5th houses, has a quality of coming to fruition. Here the Moon-Saturn conjunction rules the MC/IC axis and is found in the 5th house. It picks up some of the same issues around "serious" creativity, around history, that we've just been speaking of. Its presence in the same creative house as the natal Moon is also striking. But I have to say that the birthplace chart is more convincing.

Repeating Aspects: Moon-Pluto-Saturn

Audience: It just struck me that the Moon-Saturn square Pluto (in the 1993 solar return) is a reconfiguration of the natal structure! This has got to be significant.

Lynn: Yes, this is one of the keys to solar return interpretation. Whenever planets that form an aspect in the birth chart come together in the solar return chart, a natal pattern is being rekindled. This is strong enough when only two planets are involved, but even more significant when three or more line up. Often there is an opportunity to live these planets in a new way: a square may become a trine, or an opposition a conjunction. If the aspect is full of tension, that tension may grow even stronger during the year. This can lead to a crisis, and crises, as we know, are often salutary; they bring opportunities to look at something you have been doing for a long time without perhaps being aware of it. This can bring one of those moments of spooky repetition, where you turn and say, "Wait, how did this happen again?" It all feels very familiar, like a dream you've had before but had forgotten. A particular piece of your psychic structure is floating into the foreground, and simply can't be ignored. Sometimes this is quite wonderful, and at other times it is deeply uncomfortable. This depends, of course, on the aspect in question, on whether it repeats exactly in its original form or with a variant. Multi-planet configurations are often part of an important psychological complex. When they reappear in a solar return, even in a new combination, this particular piece of ourselves is activated. The cast of an old play is reunited for a new production.

In Spielberg's case, the configuration between Moon, Saturn and Pluto pushed him to respond to a powerful psychological inheritance. Given the connection to both Moon and Saturn, we might be tempted to relate it to the maternal side of the family. It might be a personal issue, or a collective experience of fear, terror, lack of control. Spielberg once said that the only way he could be closer to his mother was to live inside her – and he'd already done that! Perhaps what is described here is a coming to terms with his debt to his tribe, the storyteller who turns to his own difficult cultural inheritance, the story of the Holocaust. Notice the sign change – natal Moon in Scorpio becomes Moon in Aquarius. How might that be expressed?

Audience: They're so different! Moon in Aquarius has coolness and distance, especially conjunct Saturn. In the film, there is Schindler, who becomes an altruist, and the mad, scary SS officer. One responds to horror with compassion; the other becomes inhuman.

Audience: Also, if we go back to the year before, the Moon was already trine Saturn in the solar return. It was in Libra, which has to do with fairness, with how we relate to other people as individuals.

Audience: Moon in Aquarius is also universal. Isn't there something about a common humanity facing a dark force? That would be the square to Pluto. I wonder if he isn't being asked to step out of the personal into the collective here?

Lynn: It's fascinating that you should say that. Remember, the film was made the preceding year, but offered to the public (the Moon connected to the Ascendant and Jupiter) in this solar return. Not only did he make the film, which might be seen as a personal task; he also created the Shoah Foundation, which is dedicated to filming the stories of Holocaust survivors, during this 1993 solar return. Spielberg suddenly became aware that these stories would be lost as people died. I'm sure he had no idea he was about to create the world's largest visual history archive. It's a very Aquarian enterprise, where most people donate their time to work on the archives. Spielberg's subsequent films develop similar themes that treat the individual's response to blind injustice, whether dealing with slavery (*Amistad*) or the impersonal bureaucracy that could keep someone stranded in airport limbo for years (*The Terminal*).

Audience: "Foundation" is a word that brings the 4th house to mind. I would say it fits the 4th house placement of the Saturn-Moon conjunction rather precisely.

Lynn: That's an interesting observation, given that the Shoah Foundation isn't the only thing he founded this year. Have you heard of a studio called Dreamworks? It was created with two other friends – not bad for a man with Neptune in the natal 4th house, a Pisces Midheaven, and Sun in the 6th. Notice that Pluto is in the 1st house of the solar return, towards the end of the house, indicating a shift in personal identity. And I would link this to his taking on the role of producer and partner in Dreamworks, which occurred in October 1994, two months before the end of this solar return. Notice he begins with Jupiter and ends with Pluto.

Audience: It's a collective enterprise – Aquarius again. So that would explain the incredible 2nd house in this solar return chart – a new business venture.

Audience: The degree of natal Neptune, planet of dreams, was rising in the relocated chart. And it was conjunct Uranus in the 4th. That also describes the founding of a visionary enterprise.

Lynn: That's a good point. The notion of foundation is there in both the birth chart and the chart for Los Angeles. Both the birth place and the relocated solar return have powerful conjunctions in the 4th house. It just struck me that, after working on the Holocaust, one of the great nightmares of human history, Spielberg went on to create Dreamworks. Perhaps that isn't a coincidence.

Audience: So far all this sounds amazing. Is there any information about what happened in his personal life? Surely this aspect, Saturn-Moon to Pluto, indicates some kind of personal shift? I'm also struck by how all the planets of this solar return are in the first four houses.

Lynn: You may be onto something. After *Schindler's List*, Spielberg took a three-year break from directing. It would seem that, in winning the Oscar for a difficult film, a film he'd been compelled to make, he had completed a certain phase in his work. He had put something to rest and could turn his attention more fully to his private life. He began to put much more energy into fathering, being less on the road, picking his children up from school. During those years he and Kate Capshaw had two more children, for a total of seven.[6] The reappearance of the natal Moon square Saturn-Pluto, in a slightly varied form, brought change to all the important structures in his life; it brought a new seriousness, a heightened gravitas.

When a Solar Return Doesn't Make Sense

I think it's time to show you a solar return that doesn't make sense. By that I mean there's an important event that doesn't translate in the solar return chart. These kinds of examples are not unusual and they can be discouraging when we're trying to learn a technique. Other techniques like transits and progressions may sometimes be more revealing, much more to the point than a solar return. It's one of the reasons we use them side by side.

Bob Dylan had a motorcycle accident at the peak of his career as an American icon, on July 29, 1966. At the time, he was widely rumored to be disfigured, to have suffered a drug overdose, even to have died. Several vertebrae in his neck were broken, and his face was scraped and lacerated. He went into retirement at the age of twenty-five, only returning to the stage in January 1968. Now, what kind of signature would you expect for an accident of this kind?

Audience: Uranus or Mars would be strong, and perhaps the 12th house, since he withdrew from public performance.

Lynn: I would agree. However, the solar return doesn't really seem to fit. True, Mars is conjunct Mercury and the Sun, and Ju-

---

6   This information comes from "Peter Pan Grows Up, But Can He Still Fly?" by Richard Corliss and Jeffrey Ressner, *Time Magazine*, May 19, 1997.

piter is angular. We will see this again in another solar return. Again, we could see Jupiter as a protection, since Dylan broke his neck and might have been paralysed. There was an exact unaspected Uranus-Pluto conjunction in the 8th house. Unaspected, that is, unless you count a quintile to Jupiter.

Audience: Taurus rules the neck, and he has four planets in Taurus in the birth chart, including Uranus.

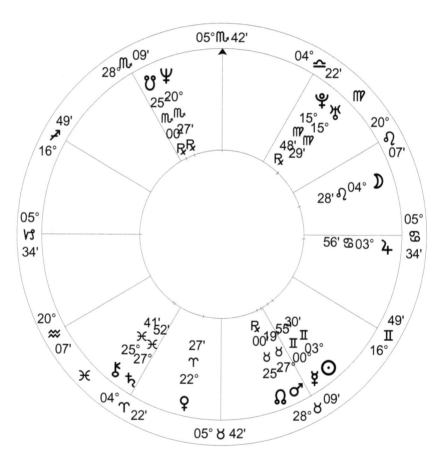

Bob Dylan
Solar return for 1966, set for birthplace

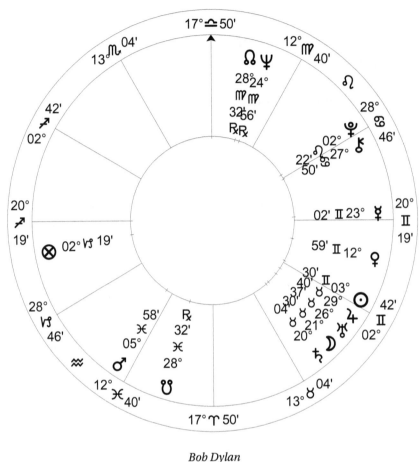

Bob Dylan
Natal chart
May 24, 1941, 9:05 pm CST, Duluth, Minnesota

Lynn: With Jupiter, Saturn, Uranus and Moon in Taurus in the 5th house, Dylan quickly became the "voice of his generation." It was a reedy, whiny, haunting voice that ripped into astonishing lyrics, and changed the music of the time for good. He was a skinny kid with a huge daimon and a wry, enigmatic take on his fame.

Audience: Don't unaspected planets like this have enormous power to sweep into someone's life?

Lynn: They do sometimes work that way. But normally I would consider them out of harm's way in a solar return like this. If I looked at this chart without knowing anything about events, I would have assumed it was a very important year for marriage, for children, and for creativity of all kinds.

Audience: Neptune is in the 10th. It could ask you to abandon something, to give up a career.

Lynn: All this is true, but I still would have expected more angularity. Now let's look at the links to the birth chart. There are many of them. The most striking are these: Mars is at 27° Taurus, conjunct natal Uranus at 26° and Jupiter at 29° Taurus. Here we have the Mars-Uranus signature that corresponds to a shock or accident. Solar return Neptune at 20° Scorpio opposes natal Saturn at 20° and Moon at 21° Taurus. This is also an ongoing transit, and it describes the vulnerability and helplessness that Dylan must have experienced in the months after the accident.

Solar return Moon at 4° Leo is conjunct natal Pluto at 2° Leo, touching into the depths, the mysteries of life and death, and affecting a profound emotional transformation. Solar return Saturn is conjunct the natal south Node in Pisces – a difficult baptism. And solar return north Node is conjunct Uranus. Natally, Dylan has a restless, fractious square between natal Mars and Sun; it repeats as a conjunction in the 1966 chart, increasing the edge, the forcefulness of the natal aspect. We can see how the solar return placements reinforce both Mars and Uranus, while the Moon is strongly affected by inter-chart connections. I would imagine that emotions and feelings were at the heart of this year, and it seems clear that the accident deepened his bonds to his wife and children.

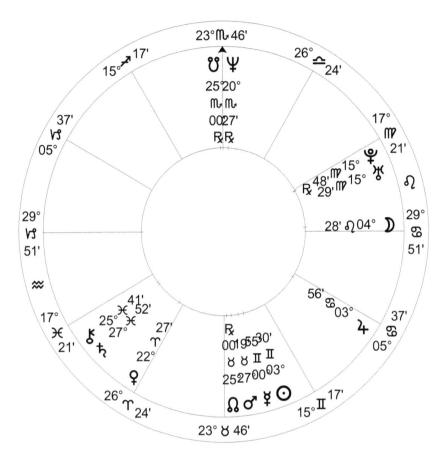

Bob Dylan
Solar return for 1966, set for Woodstock, New York

Audience: Wouldn't those connections between the natal chart and the solar return be there, no matter what the location?

Lynn: That's just it. The accident occurred near Woodstock, New York. His back wheel seized up on the way to the repair shop. See the relocated solar return for Woodstock. This chart certainly makes more sense. It's the first of all the examples we've looked at where the relocated chart is clearly the most convincing. Neptune, Moon and Mars are angular, expressing the shock, but also a wave of emotion, a need for connection and care, for a tender and quiet healing. So there you have it. It's a mystery. I'm struck by the importance of the Moon, and wonder, looking at these charts, if Dylan's accident wasn't about coming into his feelings in a completely new way, moving from the drive of success into the center of his emotional life. I am not sure where he spent his birthday, whether he was on the road, or at home in Woodstock. From the time of the motorcycle accident, Dylan withdrew from fame; he shrank from his own myth, and the glow of the white-hot legend began to fade as he retreated into his private life. Neptune is strong by transit and in the solar return, and its signature is all over the hermetic choice that Dylan made.

Clearly these charts are telling us something. The emphasis on Neptune and the Moon, and on Mars, fits both outer events and inner decisions. You will have to find your way through the geography of solar returns, to discover how they work for you, and whether birth place or relocation is the way to go.

CHAPTER FOUR

PLANETARY ASPECTS IN THE SOLAR RETURN

Trines Smooth the Way

I'd like to talk a bit more about repeating aspects in general, so that we get an idea of how they work. Let's start with something we often ignore: trines. Most of us connect trines with easy access to planetary qualities – they will stream through without much effort on our part. It's easy to think of them as natural talents or abilities that are even more available during a year when the aspect repeats. When the same trine between two planets appears in a solar return chart, it becomes a key part of the year; the world is open to your talents. Trines in the solar return indicate a smooth path, and often build momentum or strength between the planets involved. They also give grace and spaciousness. In earth, trines are immensely productive; in air they connect to ideals; in water they give fullness of feeling; in fire they give passion and excitement.

Audience: I tend to think of trines as slightly boring aspects.

Lynn: I can understand that. In the past few decades we've put a lot of emphasis on how trines can be lazy, and emphasized the dynamic side of squares. This comes from a bias in our culture that favors action over being. And although it is true that trines can maintain a situation or a pattern without pushing us to change, they have many gifts, talents, and much grace to offer. Solar returns are slightly different from natal charts in any case, and the presence of many trines might bring a welcome respite after years of striving. It's important to think about these aspects dynamically, and trines give us access to harmony – they help integrate experience.

The Grand Trine in the Solar Return

Audience: Could you say something about a grand trine in the solar return?

Lynn: The grand trine harnesses the power of the trine times three. It gives lift-off and breadth, fullness and a sense of integration. It may signal an opportunity to bring an ideal into being or a talent to flowering. It can bring a sense of joyousness as things come together, of satisfaction, spaciousness or serenity, depending on its element. Look to put something into place in the area that's signaled by the houses of the trine. Rudhyar had a grand trine in water for his 21st birthday. He found a home, in the largest sense; with Moon in Scorpio trine Mercury in Pisces and Saturn in Cancer, he sailed the ocean blue. He felt that Europe was aging and decadent, and saw the United States as the home of the new, the home for his music, for his talent. The solar return opened up the rich new world of America, with the trine falling in earth houses.

I have seen grand trines in the charts of those who have too much of something during the year – too much water, too much wind, too much fire. This can happen when planets feed the elemental energy of the trine – if Mars and Uranus were both in fire, for example. There was a series of grand trines in water the summer of 1994, when thousands came back to Europe to celebrate the Normandy invasion and Glenn Miller was played incessantly on the radio, bringing an opportunity to celebrate the powerful emotions of that time.

Going back to the recurrence of natal aspects in the solar return, a natal square that repeats as a trine in the solar return is suddenly liberated from an inner conflict. This sounds great, but it might not be. If two difficult planets suddenly find an uninhibited channel of expression it may magnify a destructive potential. These kinds of aspects may simply liberate energy that has been held back, but they also bring the possibility of transforming natal patterns. The release from internal pressure can help an individual to move forward in areas that have previously been blocked. This might be a temporary change, a green light that only lasts for a certain time, or it can be longer-lasting. In psychological work, it might be possible to follow the newly flowing energy consciously, to both experience and understand the difference in pattern. Changes made during these years can then become part of a wise use of astrology.

Sun Square Saturn in the Natal Chart

Audience: How would that work with an aspect like Sun square Saturn in the birth chart?

Lynn: These aspects have clearly defined rhythms. Remember, any aspect to the Sun is also a transit at the time of the solar return, so all you would need to do would be to follow the twenty-nine-year Saturn cycle around the chart, using the Sun-Saturn conjunction as a starting point. The hard aspects occur every seven years, and trines nine and eighteen years into the cycle. Any natal aspect involving the Sun will follow what we think of as its "natural" rhythm, although this will not be true of aspects between other planets like Mars, Jupiter or Venus. This said, those with Saturn-Sun squares tend to put themselves under pressure; they doubt their worthiness and often push hard to overcome their own feelings of insecurity. In doing so, they may actually make things more difficult. When a year with a trine comes along, it's with enormous relief – one of those times when the work takes care of itself, and the feeling of tension can lift. Most importantly for natal Sun square Saturn, it is a time of alignment between inner and outer necessity.

So the trine can be about acknowledgement, reward or recognition, with a little breathing space before the next rough aspect kicks in. It brings an opportunity to see that life can be more graceful, to walk through doors that are already open, rather than pounding against your own limitations. Because the Sun potentially brings consciousness to our experience, we may become aware that our own choices often make things difficult for us. For those whose experience of a square comes through external conditions, those conditions may ease. Aspects with planets other than the Sun have less obvious rhythms, but we'll speak more of this later.

Mars and Venus: Taking Hold of Desire

When a natal conjunction becomes a trine, we might see it as the blossoming or release of a seed in the birth chart. It will free the potential of the conjunction without restraint. And again, this could feel great, especially when the planets have contradictory energies. Not all conjunctions are alike – some blend together smoothly, others push and shove each other for the same territory in the psyche.

Hitler, who was born with a tight conjunction between Mars and Venus in Taurus, came to power in 1932, and consolidated his power the following year. This natal aspect has been described as the "love of war," although I doubt everyone who has it would agree! It does have to do with being willing to go to great lengths to achieve your desires, and the conjunction seems to have an affinity for passionate, sometimes difficult relationships. In some cases it can push things to the point of destruction. Of course, in Hitler's case these planets were square Saturn, and the story of his intense frustration over being rejected as an artist is well known. We also know that he was raised with severity and cruelty, beaten mercilessly by his unpredictable father, so that the Venus-Mars-Saturn structure in his chart became polarized by rage and a need for control, and intent on destruction.

His solar returns show Venus and Mars in sextile in 1932, and in trine in 1933. Given this context, the favorable contacts between Mars and Venus meant Hitler was able to take what he wanted during these years, but it wasn't the love of a woman, which it might have been in someone else's chart. A sextile or trine between Mars and Venus helps anyone take hold of their desire, but we must first know what that desire is. And any aspect is more likely to fulfill its potential when it is already present in some form in the natal chart. Many astrologers have spoken of this in respect to transits. In much the same way, a return chart can only deliver what is already present in potential in the birth chart.

THE REPETITION OF NATAL ASPECTS IN THE SOLAR RETURN

Venus in the Solar Return

Keep in mind that a reconfiguration of a natal aspect is in fact a reactivation of a planetary cycle. These cycles are part of the larger rhythm of a life, and each of us is tuned in a rather unique way. We've already spoken of the regularity of Saturn-Sun cycles. Perhaps this would be a good time to mention a few others.

Venus connects us to pleasure, to a sense of well-being, to the world of the arts, to beauty. It also has a strong link to the realm of finances. A close connection between solar return Venus and the natal chart can affect all of these areas, and the same is true when Venus is angular. There is probably a great deal we could say about the psychological underpinnings of our relationship to money and why that might be symbolized by Venus. Freud gave us some important insights into the way sex and pleasure, money and possession, all flow together. So although most of us are interested in love, Venus isn't only about our love life.

Venus has an extremely regular cycle of eight years, when it returns to its natal position with precision. You only get so many dances between the Sun and the goddess of love, a series of eight movements, folding and unfolding over the years in one of four or five possible signs. If you are born with a conjunction between Sun and Venus, or have strong placements in Venus-ruled signs, keep an eye out for ages divisible by eight: sixteen, twenty-four, thirty-two, forty-eight, and so on. These years will often bring whatever Venus promises in the birth chart. The dialogue between Venus and the Sun has to do with self-worth and love, with our ability to draw what we desire into our lives. It speaks to our capacity to give pleasure, our gift for delight or relatedness. As Venus changes signs, the focus of satisfaction shifts with it.

In **earth**, Venus may add the pleasure of the senses or the thrill of owning, having, accomplishing. In **fire**, Venus brings high color, drama, excitement, spirit. In **water** signs, Venus is drawn to intimacy and emotional connection. Relatedness, communication, intelligence and understanding are sources of satisfaction when Venus is in **air**. Again, we are always layering natal Venus with this solar return placement and its aspects; we are learning to love in new ways.

Even more significant than the sign is the return of any natal aspect to Venus, which often brings important decisions about relationship. These years correspond to a re-evaluation of the way we love, of our patterns in relationship. A reactivation of a difficult natal aspect like Saturn opposition Venus can bring us up against our barrier to love in such a way that we experience a complete shift; it can actually break through a structural impasse.

Audience: Wouldn't Saturn opposition Venus be an aspect of separation? Or confronting difficulty, frustration in love?

Lynn: An opposition between Venus and Saturn is likely to hone our awareness of just how difficult it is to be close to someone else. Do we feel crushed by the thought of commitment? Or are we a million miles away while sitting in the same room? Venus and Saturn in opposition help us become aware of what stops us from loving, our frustration in not getting the kind of response we would hope for. Remember, there's a difference between a one-time occurrence of an aspect in a solar return and an aspect that already exists in the natal chart. A lifetime experience of Saturn-Venus might come up for a complete re-working. It's not a facelift, it's a complete overhaul, and it can sometimes resolve the difficulties described by the original aspect.

I have said this before, but one of the most important indicators in a solar return is the repetition of a natal pattern. The natal aspect becomes very central to the year in question, new life is breathed into it by the solar return. Experienced unconsciously, this could bring a reactivation, a repetition, a feeling of fatedness, of "here we go again." But I have often seen it turn a life around.

The Metamorphosis of Natal Aspects

Oppositions in the solar return chart help make a situation more objective. The word "aspect," as many of you know, comes from a Latin word that means "to see." In a natal conjunction, the two planets are merged; they don't necessarily have a perspective on each other. An opposition in the solar return chart between the same two natal planets brings an opportunity to see something more clearly. It can even bring a natal conjunction into our lives through another person. Think back to Jeff's example. He has a conjunction of Venus and Uranus in the birth chart, and these two planets were in opposition across the solar return 1st and 7th house axis the year he met and fell in love with his wife. The opposition opened up that natal potential and helped pull the right person into his life.

Audience: What if it were reversed, and a natal opposition appeared as a conjunction in the solar return?

Lynn: Natal planets in opposition often describe an internal conflict, a struggle to reconcile more than one need, more than one point of view. When an opposition reappears as a conjunction in the solar return, the two planets involved are suddenly on the same side, working together rather than against each other. If the natal aspect is experienced as a conflict between two people, the people involved could reconcile or, at the very least, find an area of common agreement.

Audience: What about squares? What happens if a natal conjunction, or another aspect – a trine or sextile – becomes a square in the solar return?

Lynn: Squares bring action. I think of them as two sticks rubbing together until a spark flies. They will usually bring an acting out of whatever is represented by the natal aspect. A natal trine could become energized when it reappears as a square in the solar return. A natal opposition might be harder to handle, because a solar return square between those same two planets can set the conflict into motion. We could lose our balance a little. Then again, new experiences bring growth and energy – they move us forward. The square tends to be excessive. It goes too far, then jerks us back, revs up energy, misjudges our needs. But it isn't boring. Of course, you'll need to take the nature of the planets into account. A solar return square from Saturn will put the brakes on, while a square from Jupiter may be slightly over the top. Because the solar return is always based on the Sun, we are in fact looking at a cycle between three planets, with the Sun as a silent partner.

Exceptional Years in the Solar Return

One of the things I love to do in solar return work is to take a look at years that are out of the ordinary. These can be good or bad, spectacular or fated. As we have seen with Venus, some years are part of a planetary cycle. At age thirty-three, the Ascendant comes very close to its degree in the birth chart, and Saturn is usually in the same house, if we calculate the solar return for the birth place. It's interesting to note the correlation with age thirty-three in the life of Christ: an age of mastery, of realignment to the natal template. I have come to expect a particular kind of signature in those years where a person's life path changes. Often we find some rather spectacular aspect patterns.

Jacques Cousteau's Exceptional Year

Here's an example. You'll notice a striking opposition across the Ascendant/Descendant axis. Jupiter is rising in Sagittarius, and opposing an exact Sun-Mars conjunction. What kind of themes might be involved here?

Audience: The first word that comes to mind is adventure. Jupiter is very strong in its own sign, and the opposition to Mars and Sun feels very daring. I notice it is retrograde and very slightly over the edge into the 12ᵗʰ house – without limits. Lots of activity without a particular destination.

Audience: What about conflict, with Mars so strongly involved? There are many 6th house planets, and I wonder if some kind of dangerous, exciting work is involved.

Audience: Chiron is conjunct the Sun in the 6th. Could that bring an experience of physical wounding? Perhaps he is beginning to think about how to heal himself, how to heal other people.

Audience: I know this is a solar return, but the 6th house is linked to the services – to police and military. Perhaps it's the combination with Mars that makes me think of it. Perhaps he's in training; Sagittarius and Gemini are often involved in learning. Then again, it could be medical, with all those planets in the 6th house – training to be a surgeon?

Lynn: All that is very to the point. This is the solar return for a man who was in training to become a pilot. This was in 1936, a time when flying was still rather dangerous and romantic. He'd been in the military since he was twenty, stationed outside the country for a few years, so all those themes are present. His parents were great travelers; his father worked as legal advisor to a wealthy American. Notice that the solar return opposition is part of a grand cross: Saturn in Pisces opposition Neptune in Virgo forms the other axis.

Audience: You mentioned earlier about having to cross a threshold. The Saturn square sounds like some form of constraint, and that of Neptune a sacrifice. I wonder if he didn't have to give something up. Or perhaps he got lost and had to be rescued – Saturn in Pisces in the 3rd. For some reason I'm thinking of Saint-Exupéry and his plane crash in the desert.

Lynn: How interesting. I think it did happen around this time, but Saint-Exupéry was a Cancer Sun. The group intuition is certainly working today. This is the solar return of a young man who'd been in a car crash, a few months before his birthday – a car crash in which he was seriously injured. His lungs were perforated, and several ribs crushed. The bones of his left arm stuck out through the skin. Infection and nerve damage meant doctors wanted to amputate the arm. But the young man refused. He spent eight painful months in whirlpool baths, working to get the movement back in his arms.

Audience: Gemini rules the lungs and arms. As you're speaking, I'm getting the impression of a man being broken and put together in a new way – an initiation by Chiron.

Lynn: Yes, there is that sense that fate had other things in mind for him. The accident meant the end of his aspirations as a pilot, and his year was largely taken up by the 6th house process of healing and rehabilitation. But there's something else as well. Often when the Jupiter-Saturn cycle is activated, you'll find both impediment and opportunity: one door opens and another closes. The air was closed to him, and so he turned to the sea, to swimming, to recover from the crash; and he used underwater goggles for the first time. Saturn in Pisces in the 3rd opened his perception to a very different realm: the watery world. That one look changed everything for him, and he suddenly knew that his life would be about the sea.

You probably have guessed by now that this is a solar return for Jacques Cousteau, the famous French oceanographer, who was twenty-six at the time. Whenever I look at Cousteau's chart, I remember a wonderful talk by Charles Harvey on the Sun/Moon midpoint, which is conjunct Neptune in this chart. I also love the Mars-Neptune conjunction – such a perfect signature for this underwater explorer. Both are in opposition to Uranus, and he was the first to open up the undersea world and photograph it.

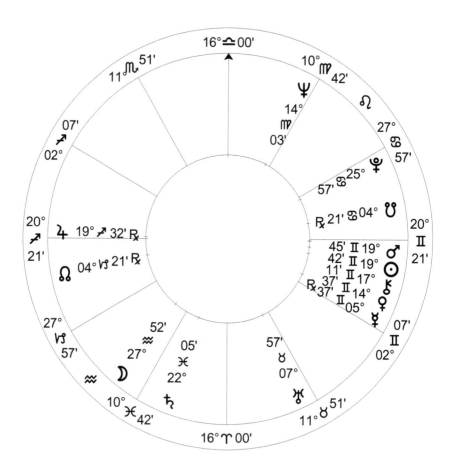

Jacques Cousteau
Solar return for 1936, set for birthplace

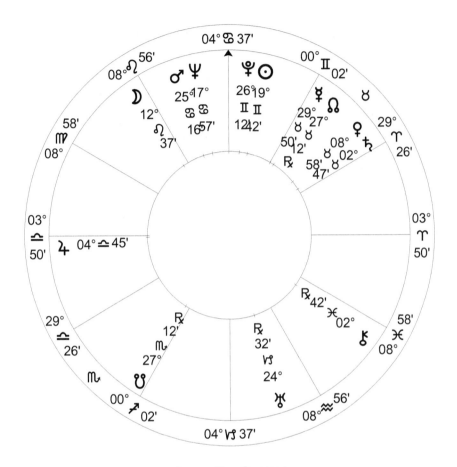

Jacques Yves Cousteau
Natal chart
June 11, 1910, 1:15 pm FROT, St André de Cubzac, France

Audience: I wonder if the Pluto-Sun conjunction also plays into exploring the depths?

Lynn: I'm sure it does, especially when you realize that Cousteau invented the aqualung to enable breathing underwater, and greatly increased the time divers could stay under the surface. He also got to be a demi-god of the deep, bringing light to what had until now been hidden from view.

Audience: Isn't there some controversy about him?

Lynn: Apparently it is very difficult to penetrate the mythology around him. One of his biographers said it was much harder to dig up information on Cousteau than it had been about Mitterand's murky past and secret relationships, and both are Plutonians. A loaded 8th house and Sun conjunct Pluto would tend to secrecy, but there is also a reason for this in his family story. His admired older brother became a fascist and Nazi supporter, and was sentenced to death after the war, a sentence commuted to life in prison. They maintained a relationship despite opposing political views, and this later affected Jacques' naval career. We see the Gemini/Pluto themes of sibling betrayal, of trickery and deception. Cousteau worked for the Resistance while his brother hobnobbed with Nazi officials.

With a Venus-Saturn conjunction in the 8th ruling the Ascendant, Cousteau may be a little less relaxed and charming than one might think at first glance. He has Jupiter rising in Libra, after all. There are rumors of irascibility, fakery, high-handedness, indifference to animals, and parental neglect. I think he became annoyed by the sentimentality of the environmental movement. But he was genuinely passionate about the sea, and played an extraordinary role through films and images in bringing environmental awareness to all of us. Like many 9th house Sun figures, he embodies an ideal, and it can be a burden for any mere human to live up to those iconic expectations. And like all good Geminis, he will have more than one distinct side to his personality.

Do you notice any connections between the solar return chart and the birth chart?

Audience: Jupiter is conjunct the Ascendant in both. That's odd. I would expect Jupiter to be a protection. I wouldn't normally associate it with accidents.

Audience: Perhaps it *was* a protection, given that grand cross. The other aspects are harsh – Mars is conjunct Sun and square Saturn. I'm noticing that Pluto is on the exact degree of natal Mars, pushing Mars to an extreme. That means it's a transit as well, doesn't it?

Audience: And Uranus is conjunct natal Venus – the classic bolt out of the blue. He was forced to give up one desire, but another came in and bowled him over. He didn't waste any time. That also sounds like something important in his relationship life.

Lynn: Jupiter is often connected with resilience, the ability to bounce back with confidence after difficult events. In this case it's a repetition of a natal placement. Not only does Cousteau recover quickly from this experience, he is also able to infuse it with meaning – destiny has other things in store for him. It's important to remember Jupiter's role in accentuating energy, heightening other aspects in a chart, for good or bad, upping the ante. The exact Mars-Sun conjunction also describes the extraordinary determination that went into his recovery. But still, I imagine the course of events would have been rather different if it were Saturn conjunct the Ascendant. By the way, this is also the solar return for the year he met and courted seventeen-year-old Simone, who was to become his wife: the Sun is close to the 7th house cusp.

Retrograde Planets in the Solar Return

Audience: I've been noticing Mercury retrograde in this chart. I know this happens a few times a year. Do you give it any special importance in solar returns?

Lynn: Retrogrades are extremely interesting in solar returns, especially when they involve personal planets. Remember that a retrograde planet first moves back into connection with the Sun; then it lags behind before turning direct and catching up with it again. It's as if something has been forgotten and needs to be re-integrated. Both Mercury and Venus disappear from the sky during the retrograde, and they also change sides, from evening to morning star. Certain cultures, like the Aztec, placed enormous importance on the disappearance and reappearance of Venus.

With **Mercury retrograde**, there is a need to go back over patterns of communication. Ideas can be less than clear, in part because everything is under revision. Mercury retrograde could signal a change in attitude toward something that began before this solar return. There is an idea of review, of seeing the world differently. And there is a need to find a new way to express thoughts and feelings, or to go back and finish a conversation. The retrograde signals a certain period of time, not necessarily the whole year, when a planet's energy is not available for forward movement. This certainly fits Cousteau's example, since his accident meant he had to rethink all his plans for the future.

Audience: Mercury was in the 6th house, the house of the body, where he must have been relearning on a physical level in order to heal.

Audience: Jupiter is also retrograde. Is that part of rethinking the future?

Lynn: Interesting you should say that; it does seem to fit. Normally I wouldn't put a lot of emphasis on **Jupiter or Saturn retrograde** since their retrograde periods stretch over many months. However, with Jupiter so strongly placed in its own sign and conjunct the Ascendant, the retrograde is probably significant. He was forced to move away from his aspiration to be a pilot, and yet this backward movement eventually led to his enormous success. This turned out to be a very positive year for Cousteau

– it led to his true path, but in an indirect way that probably reflects the retrograde.

Mars retrograde would signal a need to pull back from a plan of action, at least temporarily. For a woman, it might mean a revision in her relationships with men. It could initially feel as though the planet were weakened in some way. Withdrawal and retreat, a time of reflection before action – all of these things might be a necessary part of the solar return year. Mars retrograde suggests a need to pull back from the usual way of doing things. It could bring an opportunity to harness aggression, to step back from destructive patterns of behavior. It often leads to a reorientation.

Audience: Would Venus retrograde be difficult for relationship, then?

Lynn: Venus retrograde corresponds to a period of reflection about what is most important our lives, and ultimately concerns our ability to love. It takes us away from surface values, and there can be a loss of interest in the usual round of pleasure, in the shiny, pretty distractions of ordinary life. It brings a desire for inner connection, a need to discover what really matters.

Venus retrograde may be a bit asocial, and because we're not sure what we want, it can affect our ability to get it. Finances can suffer a bit, because we may care less about them. A retrograde often activates the past in some way, and can bring a connection to an earlier time, something we have loved and left behind. Usually it brings a deeper understanding of love, but there can be a period of disenchantment during the process of disconnecting from what we thought we wanted. It may be experienced as difficulty relating to a partner in one's life. There is a need to re-work relationship.

The Cycling Midheaven in the Solar Return

If you look at the Midheaven in solar returns calculated for the same place year after year, you'll notice that it stays in the same modality – cardinal, fixed, or mutable – over a quite a few years, pinwheeling through the four cardinal signs, moving slowly backwards by degree, till it slips over the edge into mutable signs. Those years that mark a change from one quality to the other often correspond to a shift in life direction, a change in the story.

Audience: How long does this take?

Lynn: Using a friend's example, I noticed that the Midheaven spent eight years in fixed signs before backing into cardinal signs for twelve years. I imagine this is dependent on latitude. Cousteau would have shifted from cardinal to mutable in his solar return for 1942. Although this is the middle of the Second World War, it did mark an increasing involvement with the sea.

A Solar Return Example: Sandra

This example is from a solar return that is currently in progress. It began in May 2003, and it is now February 2004. I'll show you the natal chart later, but I'd like to see what kind of information we can get from the return chart alone. What do you see? What motifs are going to be important here?

Audience: Moon-Saturn on the Midheaven: some kind of family or professional responsibility. And Mercury is retrograde, so there is a change in communication. A new way of understanding, because of the 9th house.

Audience: I notice the Moon is moving away from Saturn. It's already in a different sign, in Cancer, where it's the ruler. She could be moving away from a difficult situation.

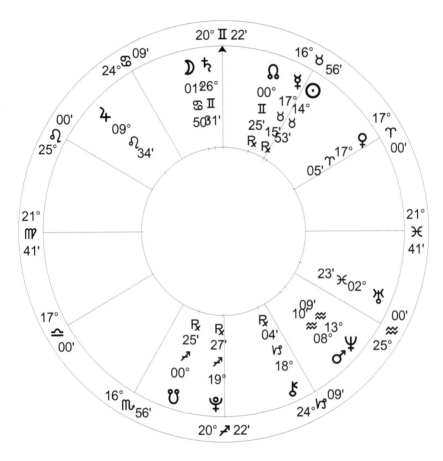

Sandra K.
Solar return for 2003, set for birthplace

Audience: The 4th house is linked to the father, and so is Saturn. Pluto is very close to the IC and the Sun is in the 8th house – this could point to the father's disappearance, even a death. I could also imagine a strong tension between the parents.

Shifting ground: Pluto on the IC

Lynn: We haven't really spoken about Pluto on the IC yet today, have we? How is it different from other angular placements?

Audience: It's more hidden, more private. In this example it's still technically in the 3rd house, so something could be coming from siblings.

Audience: Pluto here could change our relationship to home. It could feel like an earthquake, with that opposition to Saturn. Or a huge struggle.

Lynn: This is the very last gasp of the Pluto-Saturn opposition, but its connection to the angles gives it strength. Any opposition falling across this axis in the chart will point to a realignment in our relationship to our past, to our emotional security, to our base, and the effect of all this on our role in the world outside. It heightens the dialogue between our private and public lives.

All that is very interesting. I like the image of the earthquake. I have noticed that Pluto on the IC opens things up from the past; it often feels as if the ground is shifting under our feet. We all have hidden zones in our stories and psyches, and Pluto seems to invite us into these unknown places. You're right, of course, that Pluto can erupt into our lives in an overwhelming way, and symbolically it signals the end of something, but it can also be an invitation to inner exploration, to serious psychological in-vestigation. It is a strong signature for analytic work, for serious therapy. It can bring about a relocation, whether that relocation is in one's mind or a real uprooting of home and possessions.

An image comes to mind. I once lived in a duplex with a charming paved courtyard, dating from before the French rev-olution. I was friendly with my neighbors, and we had trans-formed the courtyard into a garden, a shared space we all used during the warm weather. Almost everyone was having some kind of Pluto transit and I wondered what that might bring. One day a visitor was walking through the courtyard when the ground gave way beneath her feet. Fortunately she wasn't hurt, but part of the paving stones had caved in, and gradually a hole opened up. We discovered that the drainage pipes under the soil were so old they had basically disintegrated, and sewage had been seeping into the earth for years, slowly undermining the courtyard. One of my neighbors had Pluto on the IC of the solar return, and another had it in the 4th house of the solar return, conjunct the Sun. We had to rope off this middle part of the courtyard, and then wait for months, skirting around it, until it was sorted out. Around the same time, some very dubious characters had moved into a small apartment, and it completely changed the atmosphere. We later realized they'd been dealing drugs. There were other changes: the birth of a child, the departure of other neighbors. I think that each of us experienced these outer events as a mirror for some inner process.

Audience: I'm struck by the collective nature of the events you've described. Is that typical of Pluto?

Lynn: It's interesting you should say that, because Pluto often brings in a collective dimension. But it is also intensely personal. In the story of the courtyard, the events began long before any of us came to live there, and yet each of us brought something to their *dénouement.* The hole was a great metaphor for people coming to do astrological work!

Pluto tends to bring up powerful underground energy. Every now and then, someone discovers unexploded bombs from the First or Second World War, and the emergency services need to be sent in to deal with it. Whatever is emerging into consciousness often needs attention; without it, our everyday functioning can be disrupted. Pluto on the IC could be a signature for therapy, or for family crisis, or the need to relive an event from your own personal story. You may become aware of something that has had power over your life in an almost structural sense, since the IC has this notion of root structure.

Audience: What about secrets? I've been looking at that Pluto, but also the strong 8th house in this chart, even the south Node in Scorpio, and I'm wondering if some hidden story isn't emerging in this solar return.

Lynn: Yes, that's exactly what happened. It was a year when many things were revealed in the most surprising way. It all began with a crisis involving Sandra's father – he had a car accident and ended up in the hospital on life support. Her brother couldn't make the decision to disconnect their father, despite the father's written wish not to be kept artificially alive, and then he miraculously recovered. But he was very confused. After he was placed in a long-term care facility, he kept trying to escape. One night he fell while trying to get out, hitting his head. Afterwards, the staff often kept him attached to the bed. He was in his early nineties, and during the time he was hospitalized, his children had to look through his papers, organize finances and insurance, and they discovered all kinds of things.

Audience: I notice that she is in a water cycle, Moon in Cancer in the solar return – and these are very strong emotions she's dealing with. Saturn-Moon brought a lot of anxiety, including the difficult decision whether to unplug the father or not. Pluto on the IC brought the father's death right up to the front door. But then he didn't die!

A Family Pattern: Mars-Pluto-Sun

Lynn: That's right. Now, it's probably important for you to know that Sandra has the Sun in Taurus square Mars-Pluto in Leo in the birth chart, and her brother has Sun in Aries trine Pluto and square Mars in Cancer. The father has the Sun conjunct Mars in Scorpio opposite Saturn.

Their Scorpio father had always been a very secretive man. He had changed the family name, and instructed his children to tell people they were Italian, when their origins were in fact eastern European. They discovered he had worked for the CIA. He was always a strong man, tough, extremely fit, peremptory and tyrannical. His will was absolute and his judgment final. Both his children had strong reasons to harbor resentment and anger, as we can see from the family pattern I've just described.

In Chicago, we'd call someone like this a tough cookie. We've all heard stories of Scorpios who come back from the edge of death; they have that extraordinary capacity for regeneration, and this was a father of the old school, born before the First World War. Once he got out of the hospital, he accused his son of stealing from him, of trying to kill him. At one point, he even told a psychiatrist he had no children. Now, have any of you noticed the aspects to the Sun in Sandra's solar return chart?

- Sandra: Mars+Pluto in Leo square Sun in Taurus; Saturn in Gemini
- Brother: Sun in Aries square Mars in Cancer and Sun trine Pluto
- Father: Sun conjunct Mars in Scorpio opposite Saturn

Audience: The Sun is almost exactly square Neptune. Is that similar to a transit?

Lynn: It *is* a transit. Remember, any tight outer planet aspect to the Sun is a transit at the moment of the solar return.

- Natal: Sun in Taurus square Mars conjunct Pluto in Leo (see chart below)
- Solar Return: Sun in Taurus square Mars+Neptune in Aquarius

Audience: Ah, that means that something is changing. Neptune would soften things. You just told us she has Mars conjunct Pluto in the birth chart, and here she has Mars-Neptune. I'm thinking of a wolf or a tiger turning into something much more harmless – a dormouse, perhaps.

Sun-Neptune: Letting Go

Lynn: I'd guess that's a little too harmless! You've highlighted another important mechanism in the solar return. It's as if the equation has changed. In fact, this is the year her father's power was broken. As he recovered, the nursing staff quickly realized he was incoherent. Eventually a judge ruled that he needed a guardian to handle his finances. Mars-Pluto describes a tendency to control things, and Mars-Neptune is the necessity for stepping back, for learning how to float and glide, to let go and let God, to move with the changing current of the moment.

Audience: Let me get this straight – it's her Sun-Neptune transit, and her father loses control over his own life? I imagine she was feeling overwhelmed by all of this. Wasn't she the one being asked to let go?

Lynn: Solar returns, like natal charts, work on many levels at once. Her extremely wilful father had held a significant place in her psyche, even after moving far away. To see him helpless and broken was profoundly affecting. Whatever fantasy she had of his absolute power over her was finally laid to rest in seeing him weak, unconscious and, most of all, old and helpless in the hospital. And there was another situation where she was asked to let go – her only son had gone off to study in another country, thousands of miles away.

Audience: Ah, I see. That Mars-Neptune conjunction is in the 5th house of children, so her son is going off on an adventure. Since it's square her Sun, the men in her life are affected. Saturn-Moon would be another indicator for letting go of a child. Is she married? Was there also a change going on with her husband?

Lynn: Yes, her husband had been in psychotherapy for a few years, and had changed a great deal. Now let's go back to the Sun-Neptune square. You'll see it's also square Jupiter, and Jupiter is in a close opposition to Mars, an aspect of adventure and daring. We spoke about this in Cousteau's solar return. Her son is very involved in mountain sports, and he'd chosen a school in a place where these could be easily practiced. There's a notion of delight and risk in the T-square, of not knowing what will happen, and touching into the exaltation that brings. So this aspect certainly seems to describe him. They had gone on a road trip together, mother and son, to visit schools in the summer of 2003, early in this solar return.

A Dream Comes True

I'd like to talk a little bit more about the Moon. We've spoken of the Saturn-Moon conjunction, but there's another, even more exact aspect to the Moon in the solar return. Can you see what it is?

Audience: The Moon is trine Uranus in Pisces, from 1° to 2° of Cancer and Pisces. Could the trine bring change as easily as the opposition? The story does have something in common with the example we looked at earlier, the story of the mother who lived with her fourteen-year-old son. Perhaps change is more natural with the trine?

Lynn: Natural is a good word for trines in general. But what happened to Sandra is something truly out of the ordinary. It's not something I would ever have been able to predict, but I do think we see it in these charts. Let me tell you a little more about her. I'm going to put the natal chart up so you can follow the story.

Her mother had died when she and her brother were both small children – or so they'd been told. Later, as young adults, they learned she'd left a difficult marriage, and their father had spirited the children away. Sandra was only three when she last saw her mother, and had longed for that lost mother her whole life. But at the age of fifty-seven, Sandra had long ago assumed that her mother was dead, that it wasn't meant to be. You'll notice she has Moon-Saturn conjunct in Cancer, a strong signature for emotional frustration and separation, and this conjunction falls in the 8th house.

Audience: I'm struck by the presence of the same aspect in the solar return, with the Moon in Cancer again. It feels as though something is coming round. A cycle is being completed.

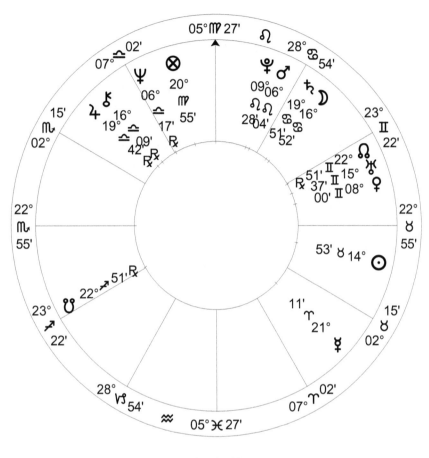

Sandra K.
Natal chart
May 5, 1946, 8:32 pm EDT, New York City

Lynn: That is the same way I would read this aspect, especially given the story. We have done work together over many years, and sometimes I don't see her for a while. Not long ago, she called to give me her news, and we spoke for quite a long time. The next day she called back, saying there was something she'd forgotten to tell me. Mercury was retrograde, and an amazing piece of news had come to her, news from the far distant past.

When her father came out of rehab, he needed a private nurse for his care. One day the nurse received a call asking for information about people with a similar name to that of the father, and she directed the caller to Sandra's brother, who lived in the same town. It turned out to be a private detective, one of many who had been looking for them over the years. And not just any detective: a psychic detective who specialized in finding missing people. This time, because of their father's accident, he wasn't there to stonewall, to lie, to put up a barrier to the search. Their mother was alive, and she had been looking for them for over fifty years. At eighty-three, in ailing health, she had finally found her children.

Audience: I am getting chills listening to this story. But I would never have expected such an extraordinary outcome with a Saturn-Moon conjunction or even an angular Pluto. Is this Neptune?

Lynn: Yes, the magic of Neptune. What is that song? "Fairy tales can come true, it can happen to you, if you're young at heart..." Her wish was finally granted. But oddly enough, Saturn-Moon is also at the heart of things. Repeating aspects in the solar return, which can also be seen as the return of an important cycle, seem to be extremely significant. There is no clearer indicator of her mother than this natal 8th house Saturn-Moon conjunction with an exact square to Chiron – no clearer indicator of sadness, separation and loss linked to her mother. Perhaps this repeating combination, close to the MC, in the house of the mother, simply says that the time of separation had come to an end; the cycle had come round.

Sandra had wanted more than one child, but it had been very difficult to conceive, and despite many attempts she wasn't able to have a second child.

Solar Return Planets Filling in a Natal T-square

If you look at Chiron in the solar return chart, you'll see that it is opposite the natal Moon and Saturn at the time of the solar return, filling in the empty space in the natal T-square. By empty space, I'm referring to the sign opposite the handle of a T-square, the sign and house that would complete a grand cross. Any planet found in the same degrees of the T-square, in this unoccupied space, will release and open up its energy. Among humanist astrologers in France, this is referred to as the "liberation point." It is something to watch for in transits and solar returns.

Audience: And Chiron has to do with healing. Does the natal Chiron-Jupiter conjunction indicate a strong potential for healing?

Lynn: I suspect it does. I have known other people with this aspect who seem to be able to distill wisdom from difficult personal experiences, to become an example for others. Of course she also has both Jupiter and Mercury involved in the T-square. And her marriage to a brilliant lawyer whom she met at university offered an opening to a very different kind of life, one she has managed with grace and attention. The distance that comes from living in another country has also been invaluable. Solar return Venus is square Chiron, and also activates the T-square. We've already spoken about the natal Mars-Sun square – an aspect of struggle, of dominance, of courage. It also repeats in this solar return, but is softened by Neptune.

Oppositions Between 4th and 10th: A Lifetime Parental Power Struggle

I'm struck by the opposition in the 4th and 10th houses, and how the solar return brings resolution to a lifetime power struggle between her parents. This is shown by the strong Pluto-Mars-Sun and 8th house themes in her birth chart. The IC is both the end and beginning of things, and here, with Pluto conjunct, her father's power was broken. What had been hidden and obscured came back into the light; the dark days were over. Of course we need to take progressions and transits into account as well. Can you see anything here that might point to this event? She spoke to her mother for the first time on February 3, 2004.

Audience: The solar return Uranus is very close to the natal 4th house cusp. That would be an indicator of change, significant sudden change in the family. It could turn everything upside down.

Audience: Isn't the solar return Pluto right on the natal south Node? And the solar return north Node is conjuncting the Sun. I'm not sure what that means, but those aspects are very exact, and they seem important. There's always a karmic feeling to the Nodes.

Lynn: The Uranus transit is clearly the key in all of this, but Neptune is also involved. Solar return Pluto on the natal south Node gives the sense that she's finishing with something, once and for all. The Node's contact with the Sun tells us that the current eclipse cycle is activating her chart, and this too is always an indicator of significant change. The whole story gives me a feeling of awe, of mystery, and I can understand why we might look to a karmic explanation here.

Audience: I was thinking about what you said earlier, about how things in the solar return need to be present in the birth chart, at least in potential. And I was wondering where all this might be in the natal chart. I was looking at her natal Uranus-Venus in Gemini trine Jupiter-Chiron in Libra. And Venus is also trine Neptune, an aspect of faith in love.

Lynn: It's interesting that you should bring that up. Some years ago, I saw a young man who had gone off on a trip to try to find his birth mother. He'd been adopted in France, and his records were sealed. Against the odds, by a series of remarkable events he found his birth mother in Canada. As it happens, her chart is very similar to Sandra's – they were born a few days apart. And he had a Jupiter-Uranus conjunction in his chart. Again, I don't want to say that trines are like magic wands – they certainly aren't – but the Uranus-Jupiter-Chiron trine holds the promise, the belief, the hope for positive change. Transiting Neptune was coming into a trine with that birth structure. Neptune often gets bad press, but it can deliver on dreams, and that's what happened in this case.

Jupiter-Neptune Aspects

Audience: I notice that Jupiter is opposing Neptune in the solar return, and making a T-square to the Sun. I know it's a collective aspect, and that many people had it in their solar return, but it also seems to fit the idea of something almost miraculous. And with the Mars-Neptune conjunction, she is able to break through to that Neptunian realm.

Lynn: Absolutely. I'm glad you mentioned that. Sandra has said that this feels like a miracle, and of course the Sun is involved in a T-square to Jupiter and Neptune, so the opposition concerns her quite directly. These collective aspects are another important piece of solar returns. They offer unique possibilities that come together for a short time, and are one of the reasons each year has a particular feel to it.

Of course, Jupiter-Neptune could also be an indicator for irrational hopes, unrealistic judgment and disillusionment, and all of this describes what happened with her father. We can see another side of Jupiter-Neptune in her son's hopeful departure to a faraway place. She seems to have experienced all the different dimensions of the Neptune transit: loss and disappointment, release, and unlooked-for blessings. We'll speak more about these larger planetary cycles and how to work with them later today.

Audience: Doesn't the 8th house symbolism apply too? The solar return Sun in this house shines light on secrets, and there are so many. And the solar return Ascendant falls in the natal 10th house – the mother again.

Lynn: I like that. Let me tell you a little more about what happened. You may remember that her son had just left to do his studies in a faraway city. Now, where do you think her mother lives?

Audience: In the same city?

Lynn: Not quite! But very close – only an hour's drive away. Isn't that extraordinary? Of course, those of you who have studied the family material know that these kinds of synchronicities seem to be part of the structure of families. We see these connections over impossible distances, connections that leap across the bounds of ordinary cause and effect. They seem to curve space and time together, bringing lives back in step with their original intention.

Uranus Trine Saturn: Opening the Structure

Audience: You mentioned the Uranus-Moon trine earlier. Uranus is trine Saturn right now. I'm curious about that aspect, and how it will affect planets in the solar return chart. Could you speak about it a bit more?

Lynn: Uranus in Pisces changes the rules of ordinary space-time, and its trine to Saturn in Cancer links it to events from earlier moments in our lives. This aspect creates an opening in the old structures; change is eased by the trine, without the need to break things apart. And change can be made lasting and permanent by Saturn. Of course, in this example Uranus is about to transit the 4th house cusp, shattering the power of the past. This is a woman who has been dreaming of her mother for over fifty years – longer than that. And the voice of her mother came to her for the first time in all those years. Uranus in Pisces has this "Twilight Zone feel" to it; it has liquid logic, loopy coincidence.

In Aquarius, Uranus is brilliant, ordered, rational, inventive and perceptive. Uranus in Aquarius broke through our understanding of the laws underlying the genetic code; it brought the architecture and development of the internet, the instant connection of cell phones. Saturn first trined Uranus from Gemini to Aquarius.

Pisces has a curved geometry – it opens up space and washes out certainties. It can bring mysterious changes that make total sense to the heart but absolutely no sense to the rational mind. And of course Uranus is concerned with freedom, and with a trine to a watery Moon, this freedom lies in the feeling realm. At first, Sandra felt a little upset at the idea of her son going so far away, but she had vowed never to impose her own will or manipulate him. Her father had been so difficult, so controlling; it had always been a struggle for her to have the slightest crumb of freedom. With Saturn conjunct a Cancer Moon in the 8th, you can imagine her anxiety about losing what she has. But she also has Venus conjunct Uranus, an excitement about the new. She said, "It opened up vistas to a new part of the world for my husband and me. We both had the impression of being released from the past and opened up to new perspectives through our son. For me this was totally liberating and welcome!" You won't be surprised that her son is an early Pisces, and had the transit of Uranus conjunct the Sun during all this.

She had confidence in what would happen if she let go. And in the act of letting go, something totally unexpected came back to her. They brought their son to his new university on December 30, the day Uranus went back into Pisces. Just a month later, her mother found her brother and, through him, found her. Oh, and there is a sister, a half-sister, with whom she now communicates regularly by email. And an uncle and cousins, living in the same city as her son.

Audience: So a sister is part of the secret. That would be Pluto and south Node in the 3rd house, and Saturn in Gemini. Did you look at the relocated chart for this solar return?

Relocating the Story

Lynn: I did. It is also very impressive, because Uranus in Pisces is right on the IC, intensifying the natal transit, underlining the element of surprise and the change in all family relationships.[7] The Sun is in 6th, which corresponds well to the father's illness, while Mercury is exactly conjunct the Descendant. The combination of Mercury and Uranus angular is perfect for unexpected communication! And the Moon-Saturn conjunction is also emphasized, because it falls in the 8th house of the relocated solar chart, turning our attention to what has been hidden as well as being a repeat of its natal position.

It's hard to say this chart doesn't work. But it's equally difficult to reject the other. Both of these charts give us clear information about the events of the year. How can that be? I don't think it's her relocated chart that *makes* things happen, but it certainly fits events. Skeptics could argue that this is simply an illustration of our ability to twist and shift the symbols to fit any situation, but for those of us who know the language of the planets, there's no trickery here, no stretching for plausibility. That's why I like Karen's suggestion of seeing them as two different layers of expe-

---

7   See the Appendix for Sandra's relocated solar return.

rience. We mutable sign people know there's a certain amount of relativity in every model, but this can be crazy-making for those who have a different temperament. Again, try them and see.

Lunar Returns

Audience: On this one, did you look at the lunar return for the return of the mother?

Lynn: I didn't. I think that's a really good suggestion. If someone has a computer, we can put it up after the break. I used to do lunar returns, but I found it was too much information to handle. When you're on the edge of important events, lunar charts can be extremely helpful, extremely revealing. Martha Stewart's lunar return for the ImClone stock sale is quite spectacular. A dramatic solar eclipse falls in the 5ᵗʰ house, and the key event concerned speculation and investment. That day has cast an extraordinary shadow over her life, and dramatically wounded her image, again a 5ᵗʰ house matter. The symbolism of the eclipse is particularly apt.[8] So much can happen in a month, and a lunar return shows how planetary waves appear and recede on our personal radar.

Audience: I wonder if, in Sandra's example, something would stand out on an angle. You said that angles are important in solar returns, and I find that, if something is exactly on an angle in a lunar return, it is often very significant.[9]

Lynn: I can verify that. Much of what we have been saying today about solar returns applies equally to lunar returns. Lunar

---

8   See the Appendix for this lunar return chart, set for December 27, 2001.
9   Sandra's lunar return has Uranus angular, conjunct the 7ᵗʰ house cusp. See the chart in the Appendix.

returns have the same areas of strength; the angles are very energetic, exact aspects tend to manifest, and repetitions or variants of natal aspect structures are worth paying attention to. The major difference is that the time frame is narrowed and focused into weeks and days, rather than months. In lunar return charts we are leading with the Moon and the Moon is always the same, while the Sun changes signs every month. Lunar returns show how we receive the world emotionally, on the most personal and microcosmic scale. It's fascinating to look at them during outer planet transits – the aspect is there in chart after chart, it colors the atmosphere for many months and years. I know that Babs Kirby and Janey Stubbs talk quite a bit about lunar returns in their book.[10]

Let's move on a bit. I'd like to give some time to the charts of the group, and we need to speak about the houses.

---

10   Babs Kirby and Janey Stubbs, *Interpreting Solar and Lunar Returns*, Element Books, London, 1994; Capall Bann Publishing, 2001.

CHAPTER FIVE

INTERPRETING THE SOLAR RETURN HOUSES

Basic Concepts

Let's talk a bit more about the houses in solar returns. In France, the classic solar return book is by Alexander Volguine. In fact, it was Volguine who promoted relocating solar returns, rather than using the place of birth or the place of residence. Volguine says that we should look at the interface between the solar return Ascendant and the birth chart. Where does the solar return Ascendant fall in the natal chart? In Martha Stewart's case, the solar return Ascendant brought out the natal 8th house. In the example we've just been looking at, it was picking up the 10th house, which we usually associate with the mother. It also happened to be conjunct the Part of Fortune, which seems appropriate, given the circumstances. So far, so good.

Volguine goes on to do this with each solar return house. It goes something like this: Should the 5th house of the solar return fall in the 10th house of the natal chart, it will favor success through children or creativity. It is a favorable indicator for those with an artistic profession. The solar return 6th house in the natal

11th would favor working in groups or teams, but the 7th house of the solar return in the natal 12th would be unfortunate for relationship, and mysterious circumstances could affect the partner. Please understand that I'm making this up, rather than quoting from the book, but you get an idea of the way it works. He then does the whole process a second time, putting birth chart angles in solar return houses. All very technical. He is basically doing a series of loops, interweaving themes back and forth between the birth chart and the solar return. This is extremely valuable for the Ascendant and Midheaven, but I find it less interesting for intermediate houses. I quickly feel bogged down and overloaded by this approach. I tend to place more importance on the planetary connections and the aspect patterns, as well as the dynamism inherent in each chart. But some of you might be used to this more detailed way of working, or particularly attracted to it. Try it and see.

The Sun Illuminates the Houses

The Sun is the vital center of the chart, the year ahead. Many astrological writers have followed mythographers in relating the Sun to the hero's journey. The Sun is both a powerful expression of our individuality and a connection to our essential self. We often speak of the Sun in terms of light and consciousness, of self-awareness and clarity. The Sun's solar return house describes the terrain of the year, and the kinds of encounters the individual will experience in terms of solar consciousness. At the core of any solar journey is the discovery of our essential nature and, hopefully, access to a greater awareness.

Since the Sun's position never changes by sign, we need to pay attention to the house it falls in. The Sun gives light. I like the word illumination, because it conjures up all kinds of things, from carefully illustrated manuscripts to well-lit halls to spiritual awakening. You could say that the Sun is bringing life and light to this part of our life. The Sun always brings more awareness to whatever it touches, and even when we're not paying particular attention, it brings warmth and light. How does it work? The Sun in the solar 7th house will illuminate the whole territory of relationships with others. It may not necessarily bring a new relationship into our life, but we will be much clearer, by the end of the year, about whether we can be ourselves with others easily or not. It is also an invitation to find out who we are by entering the realm of relationship.

Foreground, Middleground, Background

The sidereal astrologers like Donald Bradley and Eschelman divide the houses into three categories: foreground, middleground and background. These correspond to our angular, succedent and cadent houses, with a slight shift, so that foreground includes the last ten degrees of the mutable houses, where planets are strong through angularity. These authors look to planets in foreground houses as indicators of outer events. Middleground planets describe ongoing conditions, while planets in background houses – the last ten degrees of the succedent house and up to two thirds of the cadent – tend to be muffled, even underused. I would simply say they are more psychological, more internalized. You've seen enough examples today to see that the 8th house is by no means weak, and we could extend this to other houses. Whenever there are close aspects and personal planets, a house becomes energized.

The Solar Return 4th house

We've spoken quite a bit about the 4th house today, but there's one more thing I'd like to add. Many years ago, when I first started teaching this material, I would ask people research questions. Can you think of a year when you were particularly happy, where everything seemed to go well? I was curious to see what would come up. All of you must have had years when you felt things were going the way you would wish them to. I can see your heads nodding. Each of us defines happiness in our own way, so the events of these years are not necessarily similar, although love is usually high on the list. As it turned out, the years people told me about very often had planets like Sun, Jupiter and Venus in the 4th house. Now, why would that be?

Audience: The 4th house is where things begin and end – maybe with these planets there, it is the house of happy endings?

Lynn: Now, there's a thought! I don't think we want to turn this into a magic formula, but you may want to think of it as a home-coming. By this I mean coming home to where you are meant to be, feeling that you are in the right place in your life. Jupiter is spacious and sustaining. Venus can be loving and affectionate. These planets can reflect your feeling towards yourself, towards the center. I was just thinking of Odysseus and his homecoming – Venus would have been there somewhere, for his wife had remained faithful, but she was besieged by suitors and he had to fight his way through them to reclaim his land and loved ones. So we'd have to have something like Mars and Saturn as well. In many ways the 4th house is a house of deep spiritual connection. I was glancing through Ray Merriman's book on solar returns, and he mentions something similar – he calls this the house of the "true self." The Sun here isn't necessarily wonderful; it will illuminate the truth about yourself, and sometimes that truth ain't pretty.

Saturn in the Solar Return 4th house

Audience: What happens when Saturn is here, or Mars? Is it the house of unhappy endings?

Lynn: Let's hope not! This is where it is important to reflect on what the planets are asking of us during the solar return year. I could easily imagine Saturn bringing up whatever fears or lacks keep you from feeling at home with yourself. Saturn always requires work and attention. Are you in the right place in your life? If not, Saturn here can feel uncomfortable, restrictive, narrow, and this may somehow be reflected in the place you call home. Saturn in the 4th asks us to check our foundations. It may require work, but it can also be a planet of harvest, of solidity. Remember, Saturn was originally an agricultural god. With supportive aspects, it's easy to imagine the acquisition of land or buildings, even the founding of a personal or professional dynasty with Saturn in this solar return house. Saturn may indicate the beginning of a long-term enterprise or a major restructuring. It can also signal the timely end of an era, given Saturn's connection to the larger sweep of time. Some of the activities we engage in may be a response to father issues, to honor our debt to the past, or to reconstruct a botched inheritance.

Mars in the Solar Return 4th house

As for Mars, it will energize any house where it is found. Mars takes the stopper out of the bottle, so if things have been held back for a long time, it can get very explosive! Sometimes it simply seems to clear the air; at other times there is a real outbreak of conflict. I've just as often seen Mars strong in solar returns that are highly sexual, or extremely enterprising. Aspects will give us a clue as to how Mars energy is being directed. I'm thinking of an example where one man had both Neptune and Mars in his 4th house in the solar return. One day, his wife of twenty-five years announced she was leaving, going back to the town where she'd been born to start her life over again. He was utterly dumbstruck, and watched helplessly as she packed her belongings. She even took the refrigerator with her. He agreed to give her half the money for the house, and all this happened in a whirlwind, in weeks rather than months.

Now, this was during a Pluto opposition Sun transit, which had been remarkably quiet until then. After two months she called and asked if she could come back. Her mother had recently died, and apparently the grief and loss blew themselves out in this way. Transiting Mars was in an out-of-sign conjunction to her natal Uranus, and the urgent desire to leave was absolute and unstoppable. But she quickly realized she was trying to return to something that didn't exist. His solar return Moon was in the 12th, and perhaps this describes the backed-up emotions from the time they'd taken in her mother and nursed her through a long illness. There were also three planets in his solar return 8th house: Sun, Mercury and Venus. So Mars can bring conflict or upset, but it can also bring the energy necessary for survival, for creativity, for self-affirmation. It helps you to stand up for yourself. And it can reawaken passion and sexuality after a long period of dormancy.

Sun-Uranus in the Solar Return

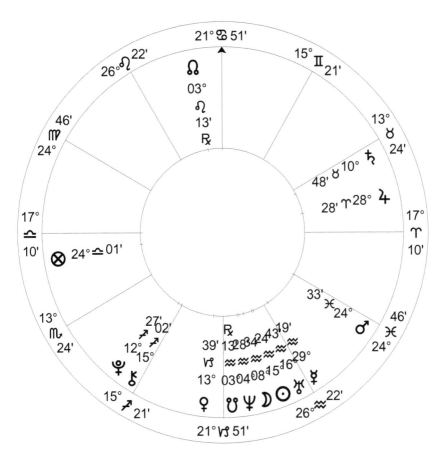

Ellen
Solar return for 2000, set for birthplace

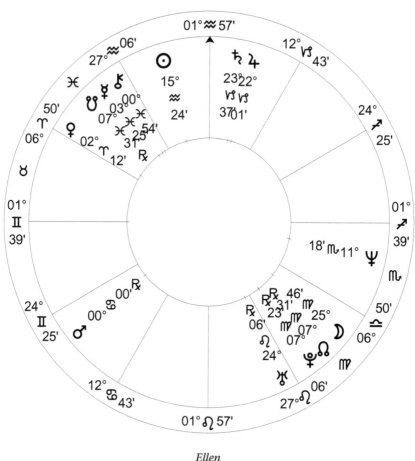

Ellen
Natal chart
February 4, 1961, 12:10 pm MET, Paris

Now, let's look at a solar return chart with a strong Uranian signature. Uranus is conjunct the Sun - an exciting, sometimes disruptive combination. We know she is also having a Uranus-Sun transit, an important event that happens once in an eighty-four year cycle. Of course Uranus moves slowly and will stay in aspect to the Sun over a period of several solar returns, but here it is very close. This solar return could be considered as the context for the exact transit. What issues could we expect to be important?

Audience: Uranus has to do with freedom and independence. Doesn't it shatter things that get in the way of this?

Lynn: That's a great description. It can also create break-throughs without necessarily breaking things apart. You could say it changes the frequency, and if you are able to handle this, it's often an exhilarating time. Many years ago I saw images generated by sound waves moving through sand, where each musical note gives a different pattern. Moon-Sun-Uranus conjunct in the solar return chart would suggest that a tuning fork is moving through the whole personality, shifting things on many levels.

Audience: I always think of Uranus as bringing an opportunity to completely be yourself.

Audience: Uranus can be very disruptive. Couldn't it mean that change comes through other people, a partner or one's father?

Lynn: That's always possible, since the Sun is a general indicator for the men in one's life. Usually we first encounter the solar aspects of self through men like the father, who play a key role in our early years; and later through others. Although this is less common than it used to be, some of us may live out our own potential through others around us. A Uranus transit can be a serious wake-up call. If we have given away a big piece of ourselves to others, if this is holding us back, keeping us small, then Uranus can be very disturbing indeed. It can suddenly seem that others around us have become wildly unpredictable.

Now, in Ellen's example there is a stellium in Aquarius in the 4th house of the solar return, and the 4th house generally symbolizes the father. It has to do with security issues, with family, with the past. There's something of a contradiction going on, since Uranus has very different concerns.

Audience: Couldn't this be a good year to buy a new home or start a family? Perhaps there is a renewal, and it simply needs to happen in that area; the 4th house could describe where it happens.

Lynn: Yes, Uranus says it is time for change, and you have described her situation quite accurately. The solar return house becomes the area where change happens. The outer planet contacts – Sun-Uranus and Neptune-Moon – put some noticeable twists on the situation. Her husband lost his job, which came with housing, so their whole situation was up for grabs. He was disenchanted with his profession, and wondered whether he should change completely. You could say that Uranus threw everything into question and forced a decision. The situation was much less straightforward than it might at first seem, since their marriage was in crisis and a decision had to be made about whether to stay in the marriage or not, to move to another country and begin again, or to buy a house in London and stay there. Ellen made a decision to recommit to the marriage, and to the ideals behind it – to make a fresh start. Her husband had been unfaithful, much as her father had been, and this brought about a huge crisis.

Audience: Does that 4th house refer to her father, then? Could all this be about her relationship with him? I notice that the Sun is also square Saturn, another father indicator.

Lynn: I am sure that's an important part of this solar return. Uranus-Sun in the 4th could be about freeing herself from the inheritance of the father. That doesn't mean it will happen all at once, and the square with Saturn embodies the tension between old and new.

Do you see how solar returns bridge that border between the psychological and the concrete? On one level, this chart "predicts" she will buy a new home, and that its purchase will change her relationship to her parents. Her parents' gift of money even made it possible to acquire the house in London. If we measure life by outer events, this chart is quite satisfying, but we can look much more deeply into things. The 4th house has to do with security and centeredness, with whether we feel protected in life, and buying property is often extremely important psychologically and emotionally. This was the first home she'd ever owned, and she had given up her life in France, her country of origin, to come and live with her husband in London. So the solar return brought an opportunity to change the way she felt about being in London, to make a new beginning. If you have a solar return like this, with many planets in the 4th, all your energy may go into building a secure base.

Audience: Will the square from Saturn create delays, hold things back?

Lynn: It could, in part because Saturn describes a heightened degree of responsibility, of consequence. Saturn square Sun is certainly going to create more internal resistance, more fear. It also points to continued work on her sense of self, on her confidence in being able to do the required work, to bring the relationship out of crisis. Planets in the solar return 4th house can wake up issues from the past that interfere with our deepest sense of security. Occasionally they test us, and sometimes a crisis brings an opportunity for resolution.

The Moon in Ellen's solar return is at 8° Aquarius and the Sun is at 15°. The orb of seven degrees equals seven months; we could expect some kind of new beginning about seven months after her birthday. They spent a good deal of time in limbo, casting about for the right solution, and then more time going to banks and real estate agents. They moved into their new home about seven months after her birthday. Her husband was setting up his new business at the same time, so the change ran through every aspect of their lives. In Ellen's case the purchase of a home didn't automatically resolve things. There is a strong connection to the Jupiter-Saturn conjunction in her birth chart – the IC of the solar return falls on that natal conjunction. This again affirms and reaffirms the idea of becoming a homeowner, but it also tells us there is a natal pattern coming up to be dealt with.

Falling on the degree of the IC, the Jupiter-Saturn cycle gives a connection to a longer cycle of time, and to the issues coming through the father. Unfortunately for Ellen, she found herself with a workaholic partner who was rarely home, two young children, and a house that could have been lovely but never seemed to get fixed up. As it turns out, her husband, who had claimed to be working late, had again been spending evenings with his mistress.

Neptune-Moon in the Solar Return
4th house: Ideal or Illusion?

Audience: I was wondering about the south Node-Neptune-Moon conjunction. It sounds so painful! Does that mean everything she built was an illusion?

Lynn: Neptune is especially painful when it reveals the gap between our idealized self and our real feelings. Ellen has the natal Sun in Aquarius. Have you noticed how strongly Aquarians commit to their ideals? She knew about her husband's infidelity, but their children were small, and she felt she had played a role in pushing him away. She felt she should give the marriage another chance. You could see this as masochism, but the situation is a bit more complex. Her own father had been a "ladies' man," and I believe she was re-enacting her parents' situation. When we do this, it isn't because we have no choice, but it may be the only way we have found to touch into a situation that holds power over both our feelings and our psyche. Aquarius, even more than the other air signs, seeks understanding through detachment, while both Moon and Neptune long to swim in direct feeling experience.

Here, with Neptune-Moon in the solar return, the dream of the ideal home, of forgiveness and redemption for their marriage, carried the day. It would have been wonderful if that dream had been realized, but perhaps it was based on a very deep fantasy that, if her mother had acted differently, her parents' marriage might have been a good one. An aspect like this in the solar return will increase our compassion for others, and over time this situation helped her forgive her mother many things. Ellen and her husband had also met in the same spiritual group, and both thought of their marriage as part of a spiritual practice.

The power of the past is also indicated by the waning cycle between Sun and Moon. The solar return Moon is 7° behind the Sun, which means that something is winding down, and the process could take the first seven months of this solar return. It was about that time that they moved into the new house. It needed a lot of work, but her husband put most of his energy into his new business. She found herself tired and overwhelmed by child care, and happiest in her studio, where she could get away from everything.

The Lunar Nodes in the Solar Return

Audience: It sounds as though she should have chosen Uranus instead of Neptune. How would you interpret the south Node here?

Lynn: I'm not sure that we can say what a person "should" have chosen. The Moon-Neptune conjunction may have meant she felt too vulnerable to risk a separation. Or perhaps she would have always regretted not staying in her marriage, if only to find out what would happen. It might seem easy to judge things from a distance, especially when it's not your life. Many years ago, during a Neptune transit, a friend suggested that maybe it was part of the transit to be led astray by someone else's bad advice. I remember feeling furious at the time, but with hindsight I think she had a point. It's always dangerous for astrologers to imagine they could have saved someone from a painful experience, or could have found the right answer if only they'd used the right technique. I really don't believe that all things are decided ahead of time and can be perceived by the discerning astrologer. They need to be experienced, and our role is to help that experience be meaningful to the deepest core of the self.

This said, I would generally suggest that the south Node seems to take energy away from the conscious desire of the personality. The Hindus think the south Node strips things down, which is not great for outward success, but this makes it helpful in one's spiritual life. There is usually a very different quality to relationships marked by south Node contacts, and those characterized by the north Node. North Node contacts feel "cleaner" to me. In the solar return, the house and sign of the north Node would indicate a direction to follow if one wishes to gain new ground, to develop and evolve. The Nodes often exercise a strong pull, especially when they are conjunct a planet.

In this chart, the contact to the luminaries tells us the new Moon to come is an eclipse. Whenever the Nodes are less than fifteen degrees from the Sun, an eclipse will occur, and we know that solar eclipses occur at the moment of the New Moon. There is that perception of a shadow passing in front of the Sun, the momentary dominance of the Moon. Perhaps the emotional issues were so strong it would have been extremely difficult to gain clarity, despite the Sun-Uranus transit. Her ideals are sucked away by the south Node contact. In the long run, this will give her greater freedom internally.

Audience: From what you are saying, I get the impression that she took on the role of Moon-Neptune, the suffering woman, while her husband acted out the lawlessness of Sun-Uranus.

Perhaps being both of these was simply too much to handle, and so one of the conjunctions got split off and projected. It's odd that the Moon-Neptune aspect seems stronger than Sun-Uranus. I wonder what her birth chart says about this?

Lynn: Natally, Ellen has a square between the Sun and Neptune, and a wide opposition between Sun in Aquarius and Uranus in Leo, so your observation is very pertinent. Once again we see the impact of natal aspects being reconfigured in the solar return. We could say she uses both planets to construct her identity. I also need to say that Uranus was lived out in her professional life. She is a painter, and her work was shown in several galleries and began to sell well. The Uranian creative spark was favored by the transit.

Audience: You said this process would take longer than twelve months. Is there any way of knowing how long it will take?

Lynn: There are many cycles being activated at the same moment in any given chart; it can take a while to sort them all out. Something to watch for is the return of the Sun to the same house. This will happen four years later, if the solar return is calculated for the same place. There is a cycle where the Sun moves through the same series of houses in the solar return. In Ellen's case, the series is 4th to 2nd to 11th to 7th, and then it repeats. Four is also a number associated with building in the world of form, so she should have a pretty good idea by that time of how far she has come. It's a direction to look at.

Still, Uranus conjunct Sun is often more dramatic. I remember one woman, Aline, who couldn't sleep during the time she had Uranus transiting her Sun. She had a business and four children, so the insomnia was getting hard to handle; her reactions were unpredictable, her mind was racing, she felt emotionally out of control. This kind of nervous system overload is typically

Uranian, and she began to worry about her mental health. As it happens, her husband was having an affair with another woman, and when she found out she was relieved, as people often are when they realize why they have been feeling miserable. She thought, "Is that all?" She laughed. Of course it wasn't particularly easy, and she ended up separating from and later divorcing her husband. On a deeper level, a separation had happened long before the affair, a separation of psyche and soul.

She had become a very different woman, and her husband couldn't or wouldn't follow. Her crisis had come as a result of profound changes. She'd been doing a great deal of psychological work, and her husband couldn't have been less interested. He had probably turned to another woman because he felt bewildered by the changes in a wife he no longer recognized. Her husband's infidelity wasn't the reason for the crisis; it wasn't at the center of what she was going through. It had more to do with her own emerging self getting ready to break out of a life that she'd outgrown. Stanislav Grof calls this a "spiritual emergency." Sometimes the impact of outer planets is so strong that people can crack under the strain. It can feel as if everything is falling apart. This is one of the reasons Uranus is associated with accidents – something cracks open.

The Solar Return 8th House

As one would expect, the 8th house pushes things to the point of crisis, but it often brings change as well. The Sun here brings the underside of consciousness to light. This is one of the reasons it often has to do with secrets coming out into the open, as we saw in Sandra's example. The same is true for feelings that have been long held out of our awareness. I'm thinking of a man who had a Leo Sun conjunct Mars and north Node in Cancer in the 8th house of the solar return. He was in a long-term relationship with a woman he adored, but they had a non-sexual, idealised relationship. Then one day she told him she'd had an affair while traveling, and planned to go away again and meet her lover. He went through a meltdown of rage and distress, betrayal and disappointment, tears and loss. But within a month he'd met another woman who was very different from his companion; they had a torrid affair, and now live together. He realized that he'd been paying a very heavy price for his idealization, that he'd been effectively castrated, and the anger he felt at her betrayal propelled him into a life where he reconnected with his sexuality. Of course the whole year was like living in a pressure cooker.

Audience: Is the 8th house always a crisis?

Lynn: If there are strong angular planets, it will usually work out in that way. In this example, the man had Pluto on the Ascendant and Jupiter on the Descendant. Remember, a crisis is often a way to break out of a stifling situation and feel more alive. If this man hadn't reacted, he might have felt increasingly disempowered, depressed, even suicidal, and he did touch into many of those emotions at one point or another. But in the end he took his power back as a man. It was the first step in working through his destructive feelings towards women, which had been debilitating, in part, because they were unacknowledged. The 8th house describes murky situations of all kinds. It is, after all, partly about other people, about the effect they have on us psychologically, sexually, financially. Much of this may be in the realm of fantasy, and planets here ask us to come into relationship with our power, or experience it through someone or something outside the self.

I love what Darby Costello says about this house, that it is the place where you encounter the dangerous side of the people you love, and everyone has a dangerous side. Emotional planets here begin to contact this dimension of relationship, and it can be disconcerting to confront it. Most of us are fairly unconscious of our power until someone reacts to it and brings it to our awareness. For those who prefer a quiet life, who wish to be left alone, the 8th house can be most uncomfortable. But again, as with any planet in the solar return, if you move in the direction the planet is asking you to go, if you deepen your relationship to it, and you are willing to look at your own shadow side, it can bring tremendous growth. The 8th house is just out of reach of the personal will. Of course it can describe emergencies that touch on life-and-death situations, as it did for Sandra, and it can be about mourning and loss. But it can also simply open the door into your own unconscious. If you have given your power away, planets here ask you to take it back.

In a woman's chart, I've noticed that Moon or Venus in the 8th can correspond to situations of jealousy or envy. The 8th house asks us to open our eyes, to own up to possible power issues in relationship. We may attract situations that help us resolve issues of disempowerment in past relationships. The 8th house can describe relationships of psychological dominance, even dependency or addiction, but these are extreme situations and would need to be present in potential in the birth chart. Solar returns can be quite literal. This is a financial house, the house of other people's money, and it can signal issues around debt or inheritance.

The Solar Return 12th House

Since we're looking at the water houses, I'd like to say a bit more about the 12th house. It is a house of retreat and calm, and often describes years where we pull back from the fray and seek a connection to the voice within. It can seem lonely if this spiritual work is unwelcome or misunderstood. But it can also feel like a tidal wave, as events and feelings sweep in beyond personal control. The traditional meaning of self-undoing is still part of this house, and planets here may feel as though they are acting without our agreement. As I mentioned earlier today, I have found that planets in the 12th often open connections to earlier times in your life, wonderful synchronicities or disturbing re-en-actments, often depending on the nature of the planet involved. Planets here can also symbolize unfinished business, something begun during the previous year (or years) that sets up conditions for the year ahead.

The 12th house in general gathers all the psychic and emotional leftovers. It symbolizes issues that still have an unconscious power to create chaos and disruption, to seep through at moments when you least expect them. It is interesting to note that Kenneth Lay, former CEO of Enron, had both Pluto and Mars in the 12th house of his solar return in 2001, the year his company fell apart. Chiron was there too, just a few degrees from the Ascendant. This combination can be seen as the rot and mismanagement that suddenly brought about the collapse of an enormous business and wiped out many people's savings. Clearly, it describes a situation that had been building for some time. There can be a strong collective dimension to the 12th house; it stretches beyond the boundaries of the individual. In traditional language the 12th house speaks of "hidden enemies," but it also speaks of "self-undoing." These can be one and the same, although, at a certain level of power, adversaries become a reality. Mars and Pluto in the 12th bring to mind those dreams where you're running and running away from an invisible menace. 2000 was the year of Ken Lay's second Saturn return. He has not yet gone to trial, but we know that a few years later, Pluto is conjunct the Ascendant in the solar return for 2005.[11]

I have seen 12th house planets bring the return of friends or lovers from earlier times in a person's life. I remember a woman, a wild Aquarian with a gift for design and business, who left her staid husband standing in the dust. She walked out on him dur-

---

11   In his 2005 solar return chart, Pluto is conjunct the Ascendant. Birth data: Kenneth Lay, April 15, 1945, 6:00 pm CWT, Tyrone, Oklahoma. Source: Astrodatabank AA-rated.

ing the late 1970s under Neptune transiting the Moon, and dove into a new life. She also lost custody of her two young boys. In 1986, when she decided to sell her business and move back to the United States, she had Mercury, Sun, Venus and Jupiter in the 12th house of the solar return. We can see this as coming full circle, reintegrating a life that had been left behind earlier. The solar return Moon in Libra was making trines to all the Aquarian planets, and the air element emphasizes relatedness. I remember looking at her solar return and speaking about the return of an old love. It turned out to be the return of her children! Her sons, now teenagers, were eager to leave the highly structured French school system and come to spend more time with her in the States, bringing an opportunity to heal the painful issues around her divorce.

The Air Houses in the Solar Return

The water houses are usually the most mysterious in any chart, and I've spent a lot of time on each of them. Let's turn our attention to the air houses: the 3rd, 7th and 11th. The 3rd house is extremely mobile. It brings comings and goings, conversations and ideas. Many planets here can indicate lots of ideas, or lots of movement back and forth between places and people. This house is also the template for sibling relationships, a template that can be reactivated during the year. That doesn't necessarily mean lots of contact with a brother or sister; it might just as easily bring someone into your life who mirrors those early childhood relationships of companionship or rivalry. We are working to integrate any planet here into the way we see the world, into our thinking and communication. Planets like Saturn and Pluto would favor reflection and inwardness, while Venus or Mercury might have more to do with the pleasure of exchange. Of course, as with any of the houses, the traditional meanings apply. An overload of planets here could mean having more than you'd like on your mind. Mars or Uranus might bring up the need to disagree, to stand out from the opinions of others. That could also bring shocks or jolts, both physical and psychological.

Siblings and the Solar Return 3rd house

Katia: I have the solar return Moon in the 3rd house this year, and it seems to go well with what you've said so far. I've just come back from visiting my sister.

Lynn: Let's have a look at the solar return chart. The Moon is in Gemini, a few degrees from the 4th house cusp, so it is straddling the houses connected to siblings and family. Like many people here, Katia belongs to more than one culture. With a Gemini Moon on the 4th house cusp, it seems to me that something might be pulling her between cultures more intensely this year. The 3rd house can very literally be about moving back and forth between things. If we add the mutability of Gemini, there is an intense need for communication, while the Moon may need connection to the past.

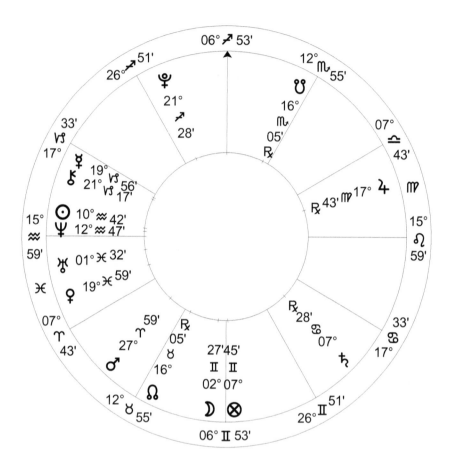

Katia
Solar return for 2004, set for birthplace

Audience: How will that work with such a strong solar return 12th house? She has four planets there: Mercury-Chiron in Capricorn and Sun-Neptune in Aquarius. I would think the 12th house would be very withdrawn, very introverted.

Lynn: She may be more aware of herself as an exile. One can be very happy in a foreign culture, but then the 12th house sets up this longing for unity, and Neptune will accentuate that, being so close to the Ascendant.

Audience: Could it be integration between intuitive knowledge and the rational mind? The Sun and Moon are in trine.

Lynn: That sounds very likely. Both Neptune and the Moon heighten sensitivity and intuition, and can make the outside world feel almost overwhelming. The Moon in Gemini asks us to bridge two worlds. We don't know whether those worlds are mind and feeling, past and present, cultural mindsets, or geographical places. Of course, when the Moon is angular it brings up questions of family, of intimacy, so we need a little more information about her living situation. Are you married, Katia?

Katia: I am not married, but I'm in a long-term serious relationship. I'm fascinated by the Moon on the IC – it makes so much sense to me. My connection to Belgrade used to be completely cut off, and now, since October, I am going back and forth.

Lynn: The Moon has a close separating square to Uranus – just one degree of orb. If we think of one degree of the Moon's movement as equivalent to one month in calendar time, this could mean that there was a change about a month before your birthday. Were you back in Belgrade for Christmas, for example?

Audience: No, actually I came back on Friday, after three months in San Francisco with my sister.

Lynn: So we have the sibling connection of Moon in the 3rd. What was that like?

Katia: It was great. It was the first time in fifteen years that I have had so much time with her. She just had a baby, her first. I was there to help look after the baby. We like each other and get along well, but she's six years younger; I left when she was quite young.

Lynn: So there is the bridging of worlds, picking up the connection with family, with the past. At the same time, the Uranian influence brings something new – the place, San Francisco, and the child. The arrival of a new family member is quite typical of an angular Moon. How has this affected your own feelings about maternity?

Katia: I felt very close to the baby. Your sister's child is the closest you can get to having your own child. But I don't think it's inspired me to think of having a child now – not yet.

Lynn: It seems to me that visit lays the ground for a change in your emotional relationships. What about Neptune-Sun conjunct in the 12th house?

Audience: Absent father or absent man. Were you away from your partner?

Katia: No, he came with me.

Lynn: Perhaps it's a shift from masculine values, represented by the Sun, towards the lunar realm of feeling, emotion and feminine awareness. There could also be a shift from what the father represents towards your mother's view of the world, but we would need the natal chart for this.

Katia: I have Moon square Sun natally – Scorpio Moon, Sun in Aquarius. In fact, natally I have Moon in the 12th and Sun in the 3rd – the house positions are reversed in the solar return. And of course, Neptune has been in transit to both.

Lynn: So the trine is a reconfiguration of the natal pattern, a smoothing out of something inside yourself, and a change in the respective places you give to feeling and knowing. But given

Neptune and the 12th, it may take a while to see what is going on. The Moon in air, as opposed to water, might point to intellectual creativity, to writing, to communicating differently.

Katia: I do have a project. I want to publish a book in Belgrade, one on psychological astrology. It would be a breath of fresh air, because they tend to be very invested in traditional astrology. And I have begun writing for a magazine there. It's the first time I've written. It's exciting, but then I come up against my doubts – can I do it or not?

Lynn: I love that expression, "breath of fresh air," for the solar return Moon in Gemini.

T-square: Jupiter-Venus-Pluto

Audience: I wonder if you could talk a bit about the T-square. Venus is opposition Jupiter and square Pluto. Wouldn't that intensify relationship, especially in the 1st and 7th houses?

Lynn: T-squares always have a central opposition: two energies which need to be balanced in some way. A third planet, halfway between the two, squares both of them, and this third planet tends to push things into action, to disrupt the balance. We know from natal interpretation that T-squares are extremely dynamic and often creative, but they can be a lot to handle. This combination of Venus square Pluto opposition Jupiter may test the power of your feelings in relationship. In mutable signs, it could mean being pulled in many directions. I was speaking to Rob Hand recently, and he said that mutable signs are double-bodied because you tend to get more than one – they are multipliers. With Pluto, it could be a deepening of feeling, but the opposition will often create tension, as if Katia and her partner have very different perspectives on what is important at a given moment.

Audience: Pluto is raw, Jupiter is idealistic. Jupiter and Pluto together are the power of the ideal, and this affects relationship through Venus.

Audience: Venus is exalted in the 1st house; Jupiter in Virgo is less open. One person could be giving more than the other, and that could be the conflict.

Lynn: You're right; the tension could be around giving and withholding, Katia is likely to be Venus in Pisces because it's a 1st house planet; it's part of what is coming through her this year. She wants to be able to give love completely, but may not feel the same response in return. With Jupiter in the 7th there can be a tendency to idealize the partner, and Jupiter is retrograde as well as being in Virgo. So he may seem too cool, too held back, or he may put all his energy into work. She may feel that her partner is overly critical or doesn't respond as strongly as she'd like. Watch out when the Pluto square wakes up. This is something to pay attention to in relationship.

Neptune shrouds the Ascendant from the 12th house side, and both Venus and Uranus are intercepted. Interceptions can be seen as a protective container. There is a sort of cocoon around it, so the planet is partially muffled. In this case, Jupiter is also intercepted in the opposite house. If Uranus were in the 1st without the interception, it might rip through and seize freedom. There is pressure for change, but the interception will hold it back, so it's less likely to break things apart.

Jupiter's Sign in the Solar Return

Most of us will have solar return Jupiter in the same sign during any particular year, and a similar quality of growth is offered to each of us for that twelve-month period. In order to interpret solar returns, or even to work with transits, we need to take these sign positions into account. **Jupiter in Aries** means growth requires taking risks, beginning something new. In **Cancer**, Jupiter brings life-giving moisture and ideal conditions for lasting growth. In Katia's solar return, **Jupiter** is in **Virgo**, a sign where it is traditionally uncomfortable. What does that mean? It means that growth happens in tiny increments, and patience is required. Unless you're a Virgo, of course, and then it will feel huge! With the opposition from Venus and the square from Pluto, Katia, you may want to go faster than the other people in your life. You may want to pour out more than they can respond to. Retrograde planets are backing away, and Jupiter is retrograde. And it's in the 7th house.

Saturn's Sign in the Solar Return

Again, Saturn's sign is also quite important in the solar return chart – we are almost all working on the same issue for two to two and a half years. The sign is reflected in both our individual experience and the larger concerns of the time. In each Saturn placement we encounter a particular fear, and are asked to respond to it in some way. **Saturn in Gemini** may reveal the split within the world or in ourselves. Any areas of duality, of ambivalence, of dark and light, can be brought into play. In Sandra's case, Saturn in Gemini brought the end of silence between her and her mother – it helped heal the fracture in her world. You may wish to look at Liz Greene's book on Saturn,[12] or other books on planets in signs, to get a better idea of how this will work.

Saturn in Cancer may correspond to a great deal of insecurity, to our fear of not being safe, and it pushes us to compensate. It can give way to a fortress mentality, but it can also ask us to let go of the past. We can see this in the collective response of the United States to the events of September 11, 2001. Saturn

---

12   Liz Greene, *Saturn: A New Look At an Old Devil*, Red Wheel/Weiser, 1976.

in Cancer often seems to be asking people to break a circle, to accept that they have no more room to grow, like a plant that has become pot-bound and will soon lose its ability to thrive. Sometimes the container must be broken, and it is time to begin building something new, or repairing, enlarging and restructuring the past. Whether it is our partners or the familial container of parents, emotional, psychological and physical containers are being refitted. Most people are asked to step out of one of them, and for some, the whole past falls away. We saw this in Dane Rudhyar's example.

Perhaps what is most interesting in this solar return is the difference between the Moon bringing in a Uranian impulse through the square, and the Sun's connection to Neptune and the 12th house. The Moon is looking for something new, while the Sun is strongly connected to intuition and spiritual practice. Neptune is happy to let things be, to drift along; then Moon-Uranus will bring things in with a jolt and speed things up. Thanks, Katia, for sharing your example.[13]

The Solar Return 7th House: Adversaries and Partners

The 7th house is one of the big four angular houses; we've already spoken about it a bit today. Planets here come through our connections with other people. They show the way to certain aspects

---

13 Katia sent me the following note after the seminar: "You were absolutely right about the Jupiter-Venus-Pluto T-square, and although you didn't want to go too much into my personal relationship (which I appreciate!), you sensed it right – this whole thing was about my relationship. We did have a crisis (actually, a few, as you said), and many ups and downs. So this is what it was about...Also, another comment about Jupiter in the 7th being retrograde – the initial book that I planned to publish didn't happen because it was not finished (actually, it's still not finished), so I had that sense of deflation. However, in November last year, another opportunity arose for a different book...Now I'm much more realistic than idealistic!"

of ourselves. And as we've just seen in Katia's example, the sign the planet is in needs to be taken into account. People can open doors for us, or bring us face to face with the less savory aspects of our nature, challenge our actions, or sweep us off our feet. Again, we need to take into account the nature of the aspects to each planet. Planets in the solar return 7th house will bring new energies into existing relationships and, often enough, new people. All this sounds very external, very concrete, but it is important to remember that it is often an aspect of ourselves that's being reflected back to us. Saturn might ask us to be more self-reliant, to hold back our relationship needs. On the other hand, it could bring in a parental figure, a task-master, or even reveal a tougher side of our current partner. On a deeper level, it would ask us to look at our fears in relationship, to see where we put up barriers, where we hold back, where we control. We may have to watch while our partner goes through a series of tests and trials that seem to have little to do with us. One of the lessons of Saturn in the 7th is accepting that even those closest to us are separate in some way. When we are unable to do so, it may lead to feelings of rejection.

Planets here can be extremely personal, but they can also be more distant, more businesslike. The 7th is important in business as well as love, and I'm sure you're all aware of its connection to the legal system. We saw that in Martha's Stewart's example. One man with a conjunction of Moon, Jupiter and Mars in the solar return 7th house signed with an agent to promote his book. She successfully negotiated a deal for him with a major publisher, acting the role of beneficent Jupiter-Moon in Libra. This kind of success helped him balance things in a marriage where his wife had been earning most of the money, and her delight helped the relationship grow.

But the 7th house is equally about relationships we'd rather not have, with people who grab our attention for the wrong reasons. Any relationship that becomes polarized, that takes up an inordinate amount of space in our thinking and feeling life, belongs to the 7th house. We look at most people in life rather neutrally; these are 3rd house contacts. When someone begins to draw the whole focus of our attention, even if we would rather not have anything to do with them, the relationship belongs to the 7th house.

The Solar Return 11th House: Opening to the Future

The 11th house opens up your connections to others, your will-ingness to embrace the larger world, and often enough the world opens its arms in return. In some ways it is the house of your best possible self. In classical astrology, the 11th house was consid-ered extremely favorable; it brought patronage, favor from those more fortunate – those who could help us achieve our wishes – and it brought wealth. It was also the house of the *bonus daimon*, our soul's guiding spirit.

Besides its usual connection to groups and community, the 11th house in a solar return opens us to the future. Remember the older descriptions of this house, with plans and projects, hopes and wishes? There's a notion of betterment, of improving the world or one's place in it. Often, planets here are imagining a possible future, beginning to invest in a new life, and much of the energy of the solar return can be put into projects that give results at a later date. It can be a political house, one that says much about whether or not we are integrated into the commu-nity. Like the other air houses, it can become an area where we project onto other people. Whether we see them as reprehen-sible or marvelous, there is a collective tinge to our perceptions. This house has a shadow side, and can raise issues around class and racism, acceptance or rejection by the group.

A friend of mine who has natal Saturn in this house, had a new Moon in her 1993 solar return, with an 11th house Sun trine Jupiter in Libra. During this year she met a remarkable number of people who were to become very close friends in the years to come, and each of these individuals came with their own fascinating worlds attached. A number of them had strong connections with other places, other cultures, and each opened doors into these worlds. She said of this year, "I started a cycle of friendship and community I'd been waiting for all my life." For those who look to soul connections with the Moon's Nodes, the Moon was just over the border into the 12th house, and exactly conjunct the south Node.

THE FIRE HOUSES IN THE SOLAR RETURN

The 1st House: Is That Me?

Planets in the 1st house color our identity for the year. Someone who is naturally soft and receptive might show quite a bit more temperament if Mars is found in the 1st house of the solar return. Mars would invite us to step out, be daring, stand up for ourselves. When a planet turns up in the 1st house, its qualities are being integrated into our sense of self during the twelve months from birthday to birthday. Uranus would ask us to break patterns, while Neptune might blur the edges of identity. Mercury says, "Wake up!" The Moon brings us into contact with our feeling nature. Having many planets in this house in the solar return means there's a major shift in the way you see yourself, and the way others see you.

Pluto-Moon: A Mother's Death

Let's look at a solar return chart with the Moon in the 1st house. Deborah brought me her solar return for 2002, the year her mother died. The Moon at 15° Gemini is in a very exact opposition to Pluto at 15° Sagittarius. Here the symbolism is again strikingly literal. There's something spooky about this in solar returns, so that, even if we know Moon-Pluto won't always be

about a death, it still gives pause. I wonder if the precision associated with exact aspects in these charts isn't a reflection of the
harmonics that underlie the astrological system, where planets
perfectly in tune send a wave through the world of form.

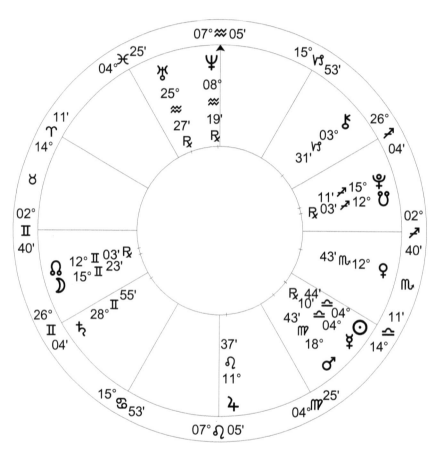

Deborah
Solar return for 2002, set for birthplace

Deborah's mother died eleven months after her birthday,
and when we calculate the solar return for the birth place, the
Moon falls in the 1st house, 13° from the Ascendant. If we move
the Ascendant one degree per month, it comes close to the

Moon, but the timing is off by a degree. Deborah began by showing me a relocated solar return for London, which didn't really
seem to reflect her experience. In the relocated chart, Jupiter is
rising and the Moon is in the 11th house. Of course, she's been
living in London and enrolled in the CPA, learning, working and
living abroad – all rather Jupiterian circumstances. But the Moon
in the 1st house makes much more sense. In the birthplace chart,
there is a strong emphasis on the parental and family axis, with
Neptune on the MC and Jupiter on the 4th house cusp. I think it
is a very good illustration of the importance of angularity in the
solar return for birth place.

Deborah: It's strange. My natal moon is at 13° Gemini, so this is
also a year where the Moon is close to its natal position. For two
years, Pluto was transiting the Moon, and when the transits were finally finished, I got a solar return with an exact Moon-Pluto aspect.

Lynn: Outer planet transits have a larger aura than we sometimes think, and when a solar return recapitulates a recent transit, it signals that we're still in the field of the transit, working
through the same issues. Pluto transits to the Moon bring a profound change to our feeling life, and I imagine you're glad you've
been in therapy these past few years.

Deborah: Totally. I would have been blown away with no basis,
no inner work.

Moon-Mars: Fighting For Feeling

- **Solar return:** Moon at 15° Gemini opposite Pluto at 15°
  Sagittarius and square Mars at 18° Virgo
- **Natal Chart:** Moon at 13° Gemini square Mars at 8°
  Scorpio

Lynn: Natally you have a 12th house Moon, where feelings are often held back, hidden away from view. Here, the solar return brings the Moon into the 1st house. You're being asked to bring feelings into consciousness. Feelings that have long been pushed out of sight will be shown to the world. What I find equally fascinating is the repetition of a square between Mars and Moon in the same signs as in the natal chart, Gemini and Virgo. This is hardly an aspect of repression, and natally it gives a gift for using your intelligence, your tongue, to go in and do battle. Mars square Moon has a certain urgency to it. This aspect tells us that Deborah is a fighter.

Deborah: Yes. But I wasn't necessarily fighting for what I wanted. I got a call saying, "This is it, you have got to come home now." Mother had a stroke, and there was talk about life-support. She had made it very clear to me that she didn't want that. Her own mother had a prolonged death hooked up to tubes in the hospital. When she told me about it, she said, "Make sure that doesn't happen to me, or I'll whop you!" It was kind of hard, because you are supposed to care about your mother and what she's going through. I had to say, "Don' t resuscitate." I was just carrying out my mother's orders, and the doctors were resisting. I had to fight my own feelings at the same time I fought the hospital.

Lynn: I can hear the Moon-Mars square in what you say about fighting your own feelings, and carrying out your mother's orders. Have you often carried out orders?

Deborah: I would say so, from the therapy.

Lynn: It sounds very hard. You had to act without having had any time to think about what you wanted or what you would wish. You were acting for her, not for yourself, and although most of us put our own feelings aside when someone we love is in danger, it is usually to fight for their survival.

Deborah: My mother was eighty-two. I think she made the decision not to go on, and she died a week after her stroke. I hadn't been to visit for a couple of years, which was unusual. I always pulled back from my mother quite a bit. It wasn't quite fair to her.

Lynn: I think you're saying the situation wasn't fair. That's hard on a Libra with four planets in Libra. The Moon in the 12ᵗʰ can be exquisitely sensitive to the feelings of other people, in part because the boundary of this house is so permeable. You may have been overwhelmed by your mother's emotions, anticipating what she wanted for you, and with Mars square the Moon both natally and in the solar return, rushing into action. My guess is that you act upon things very quickly. In some way you may only feel yourself when you're in action.

Deborah: What hit me the most was the feeling of helplessness in the hospital. It was the exact recreation of when my grandmother died – the tubes and the whole bit. It was two weeks of hell trying to sort everything out legally, and then I was at home and it hit me that I had witnessed my grandmother dying in the same way as my mother. I can remember when my grandmother was my mother's age. And now, what about me? It will only be thirty years, at the most, before I am in the same position. This has really affected how I have been dealing with the rest of my life.

Lynn: Pluto often brings us face to face with our own mortality. With Moon and Mars in Mercury-ruled signs, there's a tendency to override feelings with the mind. They may come out in outbursts of anger or irritability, or you may be impelled to rush into action. The situation may have brought you up against your tendency to take your cues from other people's needs. You may do that at work, too – respond urgently to what other people need. Are you used to being in an emergency position in your professional life? Are you always rushing to deadlines?

Deborah: Yes. And I really resent it, I really do. Clients are quieter than they used to be, but they are still very close to disaster.

Lynn: It seems to me that this solar return, with such a strong T-square to the Moon in the 1st house, was about breaking through to your own feelings. With the opposition to Pluto in the 7th, I would also look for a transformation in relationship.

Deborah: Well, my partner and I have decided to get married now, after being together seven or eight years. Coincidentally, I learned that my ex-husband has remarried. I've had to let go of the past.

Lynn: Pluto-Moon changes our relationship to the past, often irrevocably. The decision to marry may have to do with Jupiter in the 4th, building a new life, coming home to yourself.

Neptune-Midheaven: Without Guidance

Deborah: With Neptune on the Midheaven, I had trouble knowing where I fit in. Now that it's there by transit, I have five half-baked ideas on how my life is going to change between September and now.

Lynn: And how many have you acted on?

Deborah: None, because they are all unformed. It's really frustrating. I'd like to get moving.

Lynn: Staying busy is part of the defense against feeling. If you stop and let feelings come up, it gets very uncomfortable.

Deborah: That was the source of the frustration I felt at my mother's situation. I couldn't make decisions, I couldn't do anything. She might recover, she might not. She might be able to go back to her house, she might not. She might have to go to a nursing home, she might not. I had to do something, but there was nothing I could do. It was horrible.

Lynn: It seems to me that you're more comfortable with crisis than with lack of action. You're being asked to be more connected to feeling.

Deborah: I was talking to my therapist about this. In those quiet moments, doing yoga, or if the office is quiet, I will just burst into tears for no reason. I know the feelings are trying to come out, but usually I am so busy being busy that I can' t sit down.

Lynn: Transiting Neptune is now trine your Moon. It could quiet some of this urgency; it's an invitation to be more spacious with yourself.

The Solar Return 5th House: Will I Fall in Love?

We still haven't spoken about all the houses, so I'll try to move a little more quickly. When I first started working with solar returns, I imagined the 5th house was about falling in love. This does of course sometimes happen, but it isn't necessarily the case. I hate to disappoint you! I find angular Venus to be a stronger indicator. The 5th house is where we go to shine, to feel love and appreciation, and to experience the joy in life. The 5th house connects us to the heart's desire, and any planet here will be a key to living wholeheartedly. Occasionally, I've seen solar returns where someone is simply taking time off from responsibility, returning to a more carefree state. I remember one hard-working woman, a double Scorpio, who'd put herself under pressure around career and money for several years. With a strong solar return 5th house, she took time out to play, to see friends, and to dabble in art and acting. There was no big love; she simply re-laxed and concentrated on having fun. And yes, it can be about creativity and children! It is often eerily descriptive of relations with children during the year.

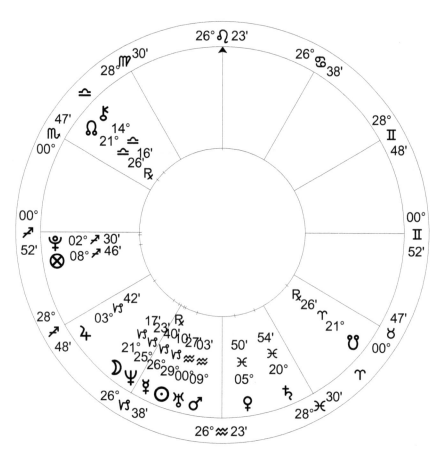

Claire
Solar return for 1996, set for birthplace

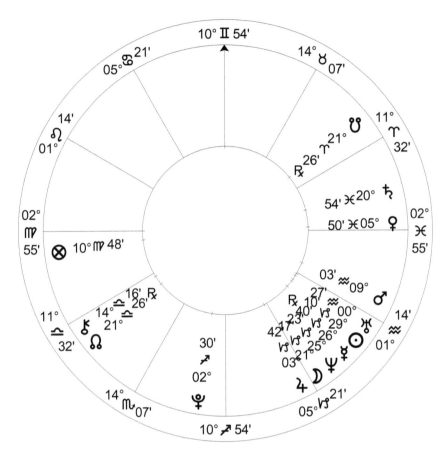

Claire
Solar return for 1996, relocated for Rio de Janeiro

Claire has given me both birth place and relocated solar returns for 1996. She was born in Kenya, and spent her birthday in
Rio de Janeiro. In the relocated chart, Venus is angular in the 7th
house and there are five planets in the 5th house. So we should
expect the year to be about love. However, Pluto was rising in the
chart for the birth place. Was it a Pluto year or a Venus year?

Audience: A Pluto year.

Lynn: The solar return for the birth place has many planets in the 3rd house. I have found that a strongly loaded 3rd house will bring to light a dynamic insight surrounding a sibling. These issues can get reactivated very strongly, and may be acted out with other people.

Claire: I can relate to that, but I'm not comfortable talking about my sister just now.

Lynn: Mercury is on the cusp, followed by Sun, Uranus and Mars in the 3rd. This is a good example for all those in the group who have Uranus coming up in their own solar return charts. I would expect this to be a year with very, very explosive and conflicting communications. Was that so?

Claire: Yes.

Lynn: And was there someone with whom you were doing battle?

Claire: Everybody. I had grave problems at work. I worked at a dispensary with homeless people every day.

Lynn: Was there one person in particular who was really difficult?

Claire: For most of that year, there was someone I wasn't getting along with. I would be exhausted and coming home to conflict. It affected my relationship, friends, colleagues. Everybody.

Lynn: So you were the bomb. With the Uranus-Sun transit, you couldn't hold yourself back. Were you aware of it at the time?

Claire: Not at the beginning, but as the year grew on, I became aware of it. I became aware of how things were enacted, how I was bringing out other people's aggression and irritability. It felt like the people around me weren't letting me be me, or were trying to make me do something that wasn't really me, and I was trying hard to hang on to my own values and my own beliefs and feelings about who I was. I felt like who I was, was disappearing.

Lynn: And was it disappearing into these extreme emotions?

Claire: Yes, for a time. I think I changed as I got more and more into astrology and those sorts of things, things that helped me express myself.

Lynn: Pluto can bring up a sense of invisibility. But loss of self might also be an expression of the Moon-Neptune conjunction. All three transpersonals were quite strong in this solar return. On an emotional level, you felt that you couldn't hold center, but other people probably saw you as out of control. Would you say that's fair?

Claire: This was the worst year of my life. I couldn't get other people to acknowledge what was happening. I had been looking at the solar return chart for Rio, and I just couldn't make sense of it, so that's been helpful. I have Moon in Pisces in a grand trine in the natal chart, and I smiled earlier when you said something about having too much water.

Lynn: You spend a lot of your time taking care of other people, with natal Moon-Chiron on the Midheaven opposition Pluto. At the time of this solar return, you were having the transit of Pluto to the natal Descendant and square natal Moon. All those emotions that had taken on so much for so long, started bursting out.

The 9ᵗʰ House in the Solar Return: Finding Our Way

All of us are voyagers in this life, and the 9ᵗʰ house is the path we walk in our understanding of the world. It symbolizes the path to God, to meaning, to awareness; it is the house of the guide and the teacher. Even when we have little interest in conventional religion, it brings up questions of meaning, of ethics. It asks why we do what we do. It can show us mere physical movement in planes and trains and automobiles over long distances, but it is fundamentally about our desire to touch something outside the self, something higher or further or wider. Planets in the solar 9ᵗʰ house become our teachers for the year, and they may tell us something about those who play that role for us. They can describe real-time journeys to faraway countries, or they can open our minds through higher education. They touch our beliefs, and may invite us to step into the role of guide for others. Planets here can help change our minds, our way of thinking about the world.

Here's a solar return with Venus and Jupiter in the 9ᵗʰ house. I suspect that the first words that will come to your mind are "romantic voyage," or perhaps something like "love of learning." There are three angular planets: Mercury and Chiron on the MC and Neptune on the IC.

Audience: This looks like the chart of a discovery. Perhaps she is speaking or writing about relationship, or about art. This seems quite inspired, with Mercury-Neptune. It could be slightly otherworldly and obscure, since the Moon is in the 12ᵗʰ. Mercury and Moon are in mutual reception.

The 9ᵗʰ and 12ᵗʰ Houses and Spiritual Awakening

Audience: Chiron-Neptune might be about healing. A healing journey?

Lynn: When both the 9th and 12th houses are emphasized in a solar return, it will almost always bring a spiritual connection, a heightened interest in questions of meaning, even for those who aren't usually interested in such things.

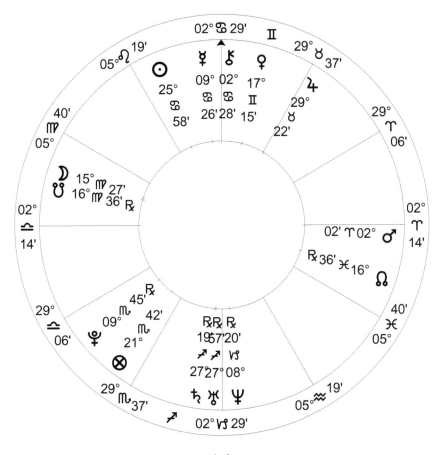

Thalia
Solar return for 1988, set for birthplace

It's also a fascinating illustration of an angular Chiron – Chiron is closely conjunct the MC, Mercury is a few degrees away. Chiron was the great teacher in Greek myth, skilled in the arts of music, war and healing. A strong Chiron can bring a connection to these subjects, or to the idea of mentoring, of being taken in hand. Neptune is angular as well, on the 4th house cusp, with its notion of coming home. This is the solar return of a woman who changed dramatically through an encounter with a spiritual teacher. Thalia is a very creative woman, who at the time of this solar return was professionally very active, involved in organizing an international symposium in theater arts. There was a considerable amount of travel between the United States and other countries. She was ambitious, psychologically astute, rather flirtatious, an emotional wanderer since the disappointing end of a major love affair. While visiting friends in New York, she accepted a weekend invitation upstate to visit their spiritual teacher. This happened within days of her birthday.

Audience: Was the spiritual teacher a woman?

Lynn: Yes. Why do you ask that?

Audience: Jupiter and Chiron are both linked to teaching, and they're connected to the feminine planets. Venus is in the 9th and it rules Jupiter in Taurus; the Moon is in the 12th and rules Chiron. And the Moon is conjunct the south Node again – we've seen that a few times today. I wonder if she had the sense that she'd known this teacher in other lifetimes.

Lynn: Absolutely. It was a very intense encounter. The teacher immediately began appearing in her dreams, and she experienced an activation of kundalini known as *shaktipat*. That meant spontaneous yoga positions, fire breathing and inner teaching. Oddly enough, a few months before, I'd gone with her to a private concert of Indian music given by an *usted*, a master musician. Thalia had found the music irritating and unfamiliar, and had only a mild interest in Hinduism. But all that changed a few months later. She experienced many spontaneous past-life memories, and had no doubt she'd know this teacher before. This encounter, as powerful as it was unexpected, brought a sudden shift in her beliefs, in her thinking, in her dreaming. She began to meditate frequently and listen to tapes of chanting, of Indian music. Many years later, it's still an important part of her life.

Audience: It sounds Uranian to me. I notice that the Saturn-Uranus conjunction is quincunx to the Sun. Could you speak about that?

Lynn: It's an aspect to the Sun, so it's also an ongoing transit. Quincunxes can increase our frustration, our feeling of being too small for our lives or minds, because they are linking two signs that have very little in common. Pressure can build as a result, giving rise to various symptoms. This pressure can eventually pop open into a crisis or a transformation. Quincunxes require work and integration. Uranus is well aspected in her birth chart; she learns and moves quickly. Solar return Mercury is opposite Neptune and in a partile trine to Pluto, aspects which underline the change in her perception of the world.

Solar Return Mars on the Natal MC

Audience: What about the angular Mars? Could that be an encounter, or a conflict? I don't think of Mars as a spiritual planet.

Lynn: I'm glad you mentioned that. It was an extremely active period workwise. She met a well-known director who agreed to help her, and arranged interviews for the symposium with many well-known actors and directors, and later, advised her in making a documentary on the history of acting. This documentary was shown at a major venue and launched her career as a director several years afterwards. The solar return 7th house Mars is conjunct the natal MC degree – a strong support for success which functioned rather literally, embodied by a man who helped her professionally. We spoke earlier about how Mars brings energy and movement. But that strong Mars in Aries, in the same sign as natal Mars, is also reflecting the encounter with her teacher. It was as if someone had taken a sword that cut through every bit of her armor. In her enthusiasm and astonishment, she went through a brief period of spiritual "crusade," and that kicked up quite a lot of resistance and rejection from her family and from some of her friends. So yes, there was some conflict.

Audience: Could that conflict between her family's values and her new philosophy be an expression of Venus square the Moon in the solar return?

Lynn: Yes, I think that's an accurate reading of the aspect. The urge to stand up for her own values is huge – she has four planets in the natal 2nd house, including Uranus. We haven't mentioned the solar return Moon in Virgo yet. Despite its 12th house placement, it is in an earth sign. As we have seen before, earth moons are productive; she was working fifteen-hour days, and describes it as "a period of self-abnegation," which certainly fits both Virgo and the 12th house. At the same time, there were two Thalias: the one who was on an exciting career track, and the one who had been stunned into a spiritual connection with herself. Perhaps these two women are also expressed by the square between Moon and Venus.

Thalia's Natal Chart

Thalia is a double Cancer with five planets in fire signs and the Sun in the 1st house conjunct the Ascendant. A strong Cancer signature, plus Jupiter-Neptune in the 4th house, emphasizes her connection to family, but with the Sun square Jupiter and Mars, she also needs to differentiate from them, to take a stand. She has an energetic grand trine in fire in the earthy houses. With the daring of Mars in Aries in the 10th house, she directed her first play at twenty-one. The emphasis on earth houses means she knows how to navigate the world of money and power, and do well in it, despite only natal Pluto in an earth sign. She has been involved in all the aspects of filming for television – writing, directing and producing. Is there anything in this chart that could indicate an interest in spirituality?

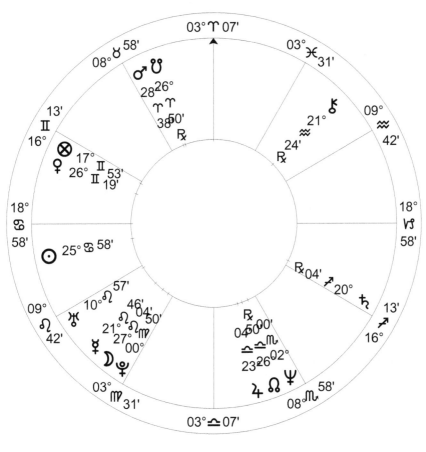

Thalia
Natal chart
July 19, 1958, 4:45 am MET, Tunis, Tunisia

Audience: The fire signs, first of all. And a 12th house Venus. Saturn in Sagittarius must be important – it is searching for something to believe in.

Audience: There's a configuration of Jupiter, south Node and Neptune in the 4th house. That could be strongly mystical. I am noticing that she's born close to Madonna, who has got interested in yoga and recently started studying the Kabbalah.

Lynn: Well spotted, that. Notice that Neptune is in the 4th house in both the birth chart and the solar return. The longing for a connection to something infinite, for a spiritual home, is part of the natal structure. House repetitions of this kind often bring a flowering of the natal potential. This encounter with a spiritual teacher helped her heal a childhood experience of exile.

Audience: I see that solar return Venus is conjunct the natal Part of Fortune. Venus is in Gemini, a repeat of its natal position. But it is just out of orb of opposition to Saturn and Uranus. And the Saturn-Uranus conjunction is in opposition to natal Venus. No wonder it was so sudden, so intense – she was having a Uranus-Venus transit, with Saturn at the same time.

Lynn: Yes, good, you're seeing the way solar returns work. It's exciting when you begin to see it. She did indeed fall in love, but not in the usual way. It was the heart opening of a spiritual encounter. As a result, she changed a great deal in the way she approached relationships with men. The transits to Venus revolutionized her values, finishing off her Saturn return with a Uranian twist. Natally she has an opposition between Venus and Saturn, so the presence of Uranus shattered a barrier to the heart. She truly became another woman. This is an example where the solar return tells the story on its own, while the connections with the natal chart reinforce our first impression. The most important of these is Venus opposite Saturn. Her lifetime issue has been finding a clear and responsible path in love.

The Earth Houses in the Solar Return

We haven't spoken much about the earth houses yet. We know from natal interpretation that they bring us into contact with the world of form in a very literal way. We connect to money and possessions, to self-worth, through the 2nd house; to the body and to work through the 6th; and to our role in the world, our career, in the 10th. What would you imagine if you saw many planets in the 6th house?

The 6th House in the Solar Return

Audience: Health issues, depending on the planets. Or an interest in healing. Perhaps a year where a great deal needs to be done.

Lynn: The 6th house in the solar return reveals what we are working on. It has to do with clean-up and repair, analysis and skill. Even knowing this, it's hard not to succumb to hypochondria when we find many planets here, because of the association linking health and illness to the 6th house. Planets in the 6th may very well work themselves out through the body, since they represent energies that need to be adapted and integrated. People do get ill, and sometimes the illness becomes the center of a solar return year, but more often than not, planets here are pointing to a particular task. Often we are put in the role of nurse or attendant. Planets in the 6th may be quite difficult without employment or usefulness, and quickly turn problematic. This is equally true for both natal charts and solar returns.

But the reality is usually much simpler. This is a house where we do the same things over and over; it is a house of the ordinary and the banal, the perfection of gesture, the repetition of a task. We can experience it as acquisition of skill, or relentless servitude. A friend of mine owned a perfume shop in Paris, and having transformed it into a successful small business, she was screaming with boredom. She had made a decision to sell, and her solar return showed many 6th house planets – too many. She wasn't going to escape the shop so easily or quickly. She had to go through another year discussing the color of lipstick, the silkiness of face creams, waxing bikini lines, another year of turning on the wheel, like a small mouse in a cage. The 6th house asks us to carry out a task, to be patient and often humble. Of course, a planet like Uranus in this house is going to disrupt those routines, or bring about a sudden change, while Jupiter or Venus could bring an element of pleasure to the everyday world. Then there's that old Saturn feeling that life is grinding you under its heel, a sense of increased frustration or responsibility, but also the invitation to invest in a difficult, long-term endeavor.

Physical symptoms can often alert us to a lack of alignment in the way we live our lives. I remember a client of mine, an older woman, who had a stellium here during a year notable for a series of back problems and minor ailments. She'd always come back and say, "I hope there's nothing in that house this year." She was a notorious workaholic with a non-existent personal life, and the body issues forced her to be gentler with herself and find a network of care, to return to herself, in a way. The notion of help, of helping others or being cared for, goes along with the notion of service and the 6th house.

Oppositions Between the 6th and 12th Houses

Oppositions between the 6th and 12th houses are more likely to signal that we are caught in a situation where we feel we have little choice, but are asked to go through a time of travail, whether it is caring for another or healing ourselves. One woman I work with, Benedicte, had a series of family illnesses and deaths during a year with the solar Moon in Gemini in the 12th opposition Pluto in the 6th. When her mentally ill brother died, she realized her sister had taken over the guardianship in order to profit financially, grabbing the leftover resources for herself. It was a reactivation of earlier betrayals, and Benedicte slipped into a depressed and exhausted state compounded by mourning. Normally enterprising and resourceful, she became very discouraged, and the next year was diagnosed with early stage breast cancer. It is probably easy for us, as it was for Benedicte, to see the connection between the difficult events of the preceding year and her physical symptoms. She chose the path of alternative healing rather than surgery, and has done well.

Natal Contacts Give Meaning to the Solar Return

As I mentioned earlier, there is another category of solar return that doesn't really make much sense until you compare it to the natal chart. I'm going to illustrate this with another of Thalia's solar returns, a chart that has many planets in the 6th house. I immediately noticed a heavyweight Saturn, Mars and Pluto in Libra, with Jupiter in early Scorpio, all in the 6th house. What kinds of things come to mind when these planets are together?

Audience: It feels heavy going. There's something important to do, almost too much responsibility. With planets in Libra, it could involve other people – maybe there's something about working on relationship?

Audience: There's got to be a connection to psychotherapy with this combination. Pluto takes you inward, Mars brings up anger, and Saturn could be frustration with the father. I could imagine a period of depression or physical exhaustion if she weren't working on these issues.

Audience: Venus is very strong. It rules the Taurus Ascendant and all those Libra planets, and it is back on its natal degree. She must be in a Venus year. And Venus trines Mars-Pluto-Jupiter, plus, it's conjunct the Moon. The Moon is in Cancer, a water sign, so emotions are important. Perhaps she's working on relationship because she's in one? Venus is trine Jupiter natally, so that's another connection to the birth chart.

Lynn: You're right, this is a year with a Venus return, and a Jupiter return by transit as well – age twenty-four. The conjunction between Moon and Venus across signs is tender and open, mildly romantic, made more so by an opposition to Neptune and the trine to Jupiter. Since Venus is on the natal degree, we know the opposition is also a transit.

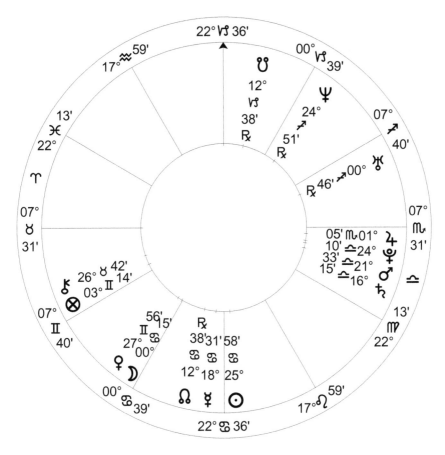

Thalia
Solar return for 1982, set for birthplace

Audience: That's interesting. In the birth chart, she has Venus opposition Saturn. In the solar return it's opposition Neptune. That's a huge change, so much less defended. So she must fall in love, but will it be real?

Audience: Sun is angular on the IC and Jupiter is on the Descendant, and that combination could be about confidence – the wellbeing that comes through relationship, since Jupiter is on the Descendant. Perhaps she set up house with someone. I just noticed that Jupiter is on the exact degree of natal Neptune. Is that the dream partner?

Lynn: Wonderful observations. You're noticing the connections between natal planets and the solar return, but still seeing the solar chart. There is something else here, though, that makes this solar return very particular. What is the relationship between Mars, Saturn and Pluto in the natal chart?

Audience: Mars is in Aries in the 10th, trine Pluto at 0° Virgo, and Saturn in Sagittarius is trine Mars. Oh, I see! It's picking up the grand trine in fire. And Jupiter is there too.

From Grand Trine to Conjunction

Lynn: Once you see that a grand trine has been condensed into a conjunction, those planets have a very different feel. The tension and tightness of the classical malefic is actually focusing something quite impressive through the 6th house of the return chart. Saturn is in the 6th house natally, too, redirecting our attention towards work. There are so many connections back and forth with the birth chart that this is clearly a significant year. You're right about relationship – she did fall in love. But more than that, she found a teacher and apprenticed with him, learning the craft of acting and directing, working with actors. She had won a travel scholarship for work and study in New York, so she arrived under positive auspices, very close to her birthday. When she arrived, she did the round of acting schools and chose the best. She threw herself into the work completely, becoming the teacher's assistant. It was a year of many significant and warm friendships, one of the best in her life, and she felt she'd "come home" as soon as she arrived in New York. And yes, she did begin therapy. There was a lot of work to do on her father issues.

Audience: Was she involved with an older man?

Lynn: Why do you ask that?

Audience: Venus is opposition Saturn in the birth chart, for one thing. And she has Capricorn on the 7th house cusp. You mentioned father issues just now.

Lynn: Yes, it was an older man, one she admired a great deal. The love affair was very passionate, and I believe it was the first time she let herself be swept away – not surprising, with the Neptune transit. As one might expect with the Venus opposition Neptune aspect across the 2nd/8th axis, it was extremely erotic and sensual. It didn't turn out to be exactly what she'd hoped for, and that, too, is part of Neptune, but it remained one of the important love stories in her life. This is an example where the birth chart and the solar return together give the full meaning to the year.

The Solar Return 10th House: Taking Direction

The 10th house is a place of decision-making. Its angularity means that solar return planets here have high visibility, and we encounter them as we step out into the world. Jupiter may ask us to step into a leading role, to take up more room, to be generous or sanguine, to be a teacher or a role model for success. Or we may mysteriously draw these kinds of people into our lives. The 10th house is a house that is partly outside; it is our interface with the world at large. In classical astrology it is the house of the ruler, the king, the president. These days it more often describes supervisors and managers, our parents, and more specifically the mother, and it can connote people in the government, and our attitude towards them. We can easily project our issues around control onto those symbolized by the planets in this house.

10th house planets help make us aware of what has authority over our lives, and to what we give our authority. In reality, any planet in the 10th house of the solar return is asking something of us, and giving us direction for the year. We can see these planets as the energies that hold the rudder for the solar return year, that steer us into the time ahead. The 10th house also has an association with the goddess Fortuna, with the vagaries of fate and destiny. Let's do a quick run-through of solar return planets in the 10th house.

The Sun helps us step into our own authority, or brings a role model we can admire. It will bring light to our path in life, make our direction clearer and stronger. It can lift us to a peak of achievement and recognition.

The Moon asks us to let feeling be our guide, to accept change and movement. We may find our direction from a feminine figure, our mother, or another woman in our life. We can slip into the role of caretaker, or show our vulnerability, our sensitivity to the world.

Mercury comes as a go-between or a trickster, opens channels of communication, and activates inventiveness. Deals are made, people are met, and ideas come winging through.

Venus offers us the gift of relatedness, the ability to make the world kinder or more beautiful, and may open our life to love.

Mars may propel us into the world and prod us to take charge, but it can also ask us to fight our way through constraints. We have the energy and strength to accomplish our goals and we manage to impose our desires.

Jupiter invites us to step into a larger role, to act with benevolence, with generosity towards others, to be open to what comes our way. Recognition may come easily. Jupiter often brings success or satisfaction, and life seems smooth.

Saturn can make us aware of commitments, requirements or responsibilities, and it has a way of jacking up the pressure, but it can also indicate a year of major accomplishment, if we can handle the strain.

Chiron often leads us away from the beaten track; we may step out of bounds, seek new understanding, or be involved in taking others under our tutelage. Chiron calls us to healing adventures, or asks us to tend to those who need healing.

Uranus can bring a breakthrough or shatter what we have patiently built, as it did in Martha Stewart's example. It can ask us to change, or open a new pathway.

Neptune asks us to let dreams and intuition lead the way, but we can be caught by glamor, read the wrong signs, and lose our way. We follow the path of the ideal, the irrational or the mystical, and sometimes move onto a spiritual path.

Pluto can bring far-reaching change or lasting power, especially close to the cusp. It can also wipe out whatever keeps us from following our true calling – not that we necessarily understand this process at the time.

Most of us immediately think of career when it comes to this house, but it always carries a larger sense of connection to purpose, and anything that gets in the way of this can also be symbolized by this house. Planets here may ask us to take on a particular role, or confront our resistance to authority. In general, planets in the earth houses will bring visible results if we work with their energies.

The 2nd House in the Solar Return

Most of us think of financial issues when we come to the 2nd house, and this can also be true of the solar return. This is a house where we touch into our sense of self-esteem, of what we have, what we are worth, and we often look for a reflection in the material world. The ancients referred to this house as a doorway that led back out from the underworld. I love this image of emerging into a world of smell and sense and form after a time in the dark. Our body is awakened; there's a delight in touch and taste, in the possibility of life in all its physicality. In Thalia's solar return for 1982, a year of great eroticism, both Moon and Venus fell in the 2nd house, she was building confidence in herself as a woman and as an artist. This house is sometimes connected to talents and shows what we have to offer to others.

Planets here reveal what we can bring to the year, what may be planted and yield results. One man stepped into fatherhood with the Moon in the 2nd house of the solar return, and discovered his ability to care for others. We build substance using the qualities of planets in the solar return 2nd house. Another woman with a conjunction of Mars and Pluto in Sagittarius in the solar 2nd house invested considerable time and resources in a business project involving travel and teaching. The qualities she is being asked to develop have to do with initiative and passion.

Planets in the solar return 2nd house can also describe issues that need work before we can feel we have something to offer. Saturn in the 2nd could indicate less favorable conditions for building wealth, or awaken our fear of poverty. It might also ask us to build for the long term, to invest in time, to measure and weigh our resources.

There is much more to say about solar returns, much more to explore. If you work with them, they will help you connect to the sky of the moment, and the way we come into contact with ever-changing planetary patterns. I hope you've got a sense of how to interpret solar returns, what to watch for, where to go with the information you find. I would suggest you look up the charts for important years in your life, and see how they speak to you. Look at years of joy and years of sorrow. Then look to the future and see what you can find.

Appendix

STEPS FOR SOLAR RETURN INTERPRETATION

Interpretation Steps Part 1

- Look at the planetary distribution? Is it similar or dissimilar to the natal pattern? Is there a pattern like a bowl, bundle, splash? Your energy will be correspondingly bigger or tighter during the year.
- Which houses are particularly emphasized? These describe charged areas of experience for the solar return year. The Sun brings its light and focus to whatever house it occupies in the solar return.
- What is the relationship between the Sun and Moon? The Lunation cycle will describe a quality of unfolding.
- Look at the Moon's element, and determine how many years it will stay in this element. Note the strength or weakness of this element in the natal chart. Is it familiar or unfamiliar?
- Take note of any precise aspects between planets. These will be very active during the year.
- Planets conjunct the angles will carry the year's dominant themes.
- Which planets are in angular houses? They will tend to be strongly visible during the solar return year.

Interpretation Steps Part 2

- Where does the solar return Ascendant fall in the natal chart? This natal house will represent a key theme during the year.
- Where does the solar return MC fall in the natal chart? It will describe an area of life which is being developed during the year.
- Go through the natal planets one by one. Do any solar return planets fall on the same degree (or within a 3-degree orb)? These planets will act as agents for the natal planet during the solar return year.
- Go through the natal houses and see whether any solar return planets fall in the same houses in the solar return. This kind of correlation brings the planet into strong focus.
- Make a list of aspects in the solar return and compare them to natal aspects. Are there any repetitions or similarities? For example, a natal Saturn opposition Venus may reappear as a conjunction in the solar return. These repetitions can be seen as an important unfolding of the natal aspect and an opportunity to experience the aspect from a slightly different perspective. When the aspect is the same as in the birthchart it can activate an individual's fundamental relationship with the planets in question, and even indicate a year of destiny where a natal pattern is lived out.

EXAMPLES OF SOLAR AND LUNAR RETURNS

Example 1: Sigmund Freud, Solar Return for 1906

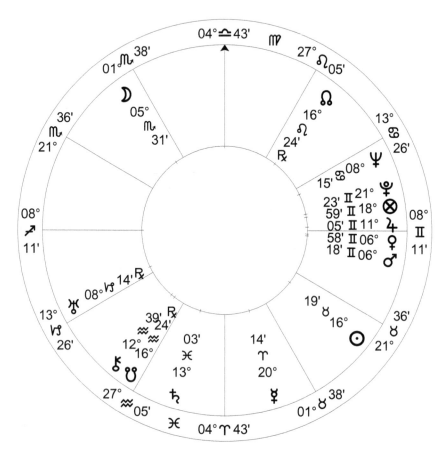

Sigmund Freud
Solar return for 1906, set for birthplace

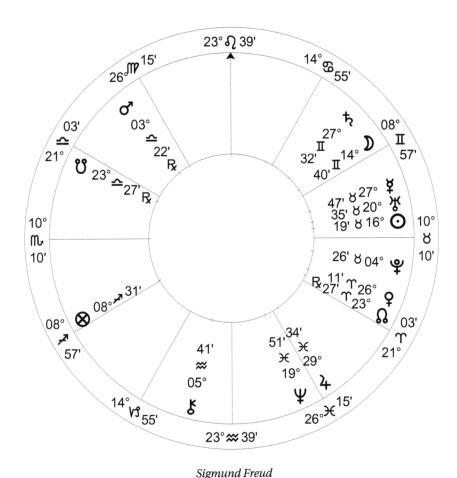

Sigmund Freud
Birth Chart
May 6, 1856, 6:30 pm LMT, Freiburg (Príbor), Moravia (Czech Republic)

What to Look For?

An exciting stellium starts at the cusp of the 7th house of this solar return chart, with Mars, Venus, Jupiter and Pluto in Gemini, followed by Neptune in Cancer. Stelliums are often difficult to interpret in solar returns, because they bring so much information to the same area of life. A passionate encounter is likely here, with overtones of love and rivalry seen in the exact conjunction of Mars and Venus. Jupiter adds openness to the conjunction, bringing enthusiasm to Eros. It can constellate the archetype of the benefactor, the teacher, or the guide. We may meet someone who opens up our world, or be in a position of generosity toward others. Mars conjunct Jupiter can be an aspect of victory and conquest, of successful effort, and could bring an active alliance. The emphasis on Gemini tells us to look to communication, to ideas and words as a key element in the exchange with others. Pluto and Neptune further along in this house indicate larger unconscious themes that are operating under the surface; they may draw in the archetypes of both betrayer and savior, and point to strong collective themes in a given partnership.

Freud has a natal opposition between Mars in Libra and Jupiter in late Pisces, across the 5th and 11th houses. We can see this as his struggle to break through social convention, and particularly the impulse to convey the importance of sexuality. This natal aspect reflects the often hostile responses directed towards his work, and the battle to win acceptance for his ideas. It hints at a possible struggle with rejection, at flare ups in relationships with friends and colleagues, and at a need to be recognized for his individuality, his wisdom and his genius. This aspect reappears as a conjunction in the solar return, giving an opportunity to resolve the natal conflict, to find a relationship of shared belief. There is a new conscript, someone who may be drafted into the movement, or carried along by the juggernaut of ideas and passion. This may be the ideal sparring partner, a brother-in-arms, or an attractive, potentially dangerous rival. Since natal Jupiter is in the 5th, it could also bring an encounter with a spiritual heir.

The solar return Moon is close to the natal Ascendant - feelings will be a key to the year. In the solar return 11th house, it brings emotional overtones to friendship; it could even symbolize the adoption of a child into the tribe. There is a possibility of real intimacy in a non-sexual relationship, but the Moon can also attract situations of dependency. The Moon in Scorpio has an anxious edge, which is soothed by the grand trine to Neptune and Saturn in water, an aspect of idealized feeling, of emotional understanding. There may be an opportunity to heal feelings of rejection or dislike from the community at large.

Jupiter is conjunct the natal Moon, another signature for emotional expansiveness and intimacy. Generous and warm, offering an invitation to the inner life, Jupiter is nonetheless square a more reticent Saturn in the 3rd house. There may be an unsuccessful attempt to control communication. Feelings of reserve and distance could alternate with the evident attraction and warmth. Saturn also squares Mars and Venus, and reflects an attitude of intellectual caution towards the strong passion of the conjunction.

What Happened?

Freud and Jung began an exchange of letters a few months before this solar return began, and it quickly accelerated into a passionate exchange of ideas. They met in February/March 1907, when Jung traveled to Vienna on Freud's invitation. They were at first enchanted with each other, mutually delighted and inspired. Jung was Freud's first non-Jewish disciple, and it has been suggested that Freud saw the younger man as a possible heir apparent, a vehicle for his ideas to break through to a wider audience. Freud was attracted to Jung's brilliance and promise, but over time elements of rivalry began to creep into their relationship. It is interesting to speculate on whether this solar return already contains the seeds of the longer-term relationship, which ended in 1912 in mutual disappointment. Both men had natal Uranus in the 7th house, and both needed to be acknowledged for their unique contributions.

Example 2: Carl Gustav Jung, Solar Return for 1906

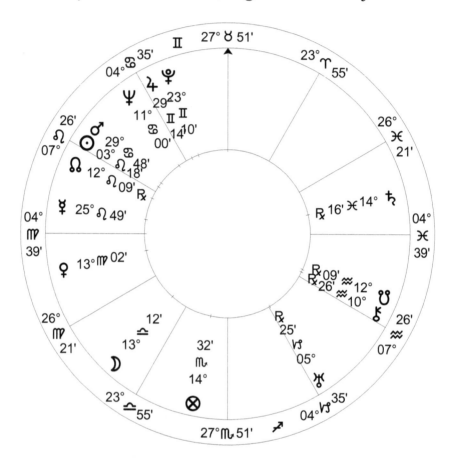

Carl Gustav Jung
Solar return for 1906, set for birthplace

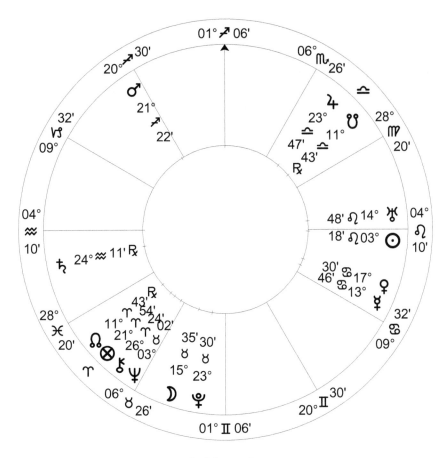

Carl Gustav Jung
Birth Chart
July 26, 1875, 7:32 pm SZOT, Kesswil, Switzerland

What to Look For?

Saturn in the 7ᵗʰ house of the solar return means we must take relationship seriously. With Saturn opposition Venus in the 1ˢᵗ, there may be a combination of fear and seduction, a notion of commitment and accompanying constraint. Venus could play the role of charmer to Saturn's gruff authority. Or there could be a relationship between those of unequal age and status - a "May to December" wedding. Saturn may constellate the father and can bring to life unresolved issues from childhood, a need for someone to incarnate authority. Saturn in Pisces is unlikely to completely satisfy, and Venus in Virgo might be particularly demanding. Respect and fear, responsibility and authority will all enter into a demanding relationship. In Jung's natal chart, Saturn is in the 1st house Aquarius, which asks him to embody the role of an enlightened father figure. This year brings an unusual reversal of the natal pattern, suggesting that he is seeking to encounter an aspect of himself through another person.

The Sun is conjunct Mars in the Solar Return, indicating a drive for self-affirmation. In the 11th house, it brings a position of strength or leadership to any group affiliation, although any lack of clarity could lead to conflict. Mars is also in the 11th house natally (as it is for Freud), and in the solar return chart gives an opportunity to fulfill the natal potential.

The solar return Ascendant falls in the natal 7th house, again placing the emphasis on relationship. Virgo on the Ascendant could describe a certain self-effacement, the role of the humble petitioner. With Mercury in the 12th a collective impulse underlies the events of the year, and brings a desire to explore the non-rational dimension of life.

Solar return north Node conjuncts natal Uranus in the 7th, a green light to enter into an odd fellowship, an unlikely match. There is an invitation to claim one's difference, to step into the position of iconoclast, to be oneself no matter what the cost. Solar return Moon in Libra is conjunct the natal south node, bringing a sense of *déjà vu*, a feeling of instant familiarity. It strengthens a tendency to keep things agreeable or harmonious. The natal south Node in Libra warns against too much compromise.

What Happened?

Jung entered into a writing relationship with Freud, the "father of psychoanalysis," and found himself treated with filial regard and professional encouragement. Freud was fifty, Jung was thirty-one and already successful. Given his natal Uranus in the 7th, this may have been the only time that he allowed another to take on this role for him, since even as a child he turned away from his own father's spiritual authority. If this was a love affair, it's clear that the emotions were not the same for Freud as they were for Jung. Freud's solar Return has all the indications of real warmth and passion, while Jung's solar return shows more reserve, greater respect, and issues of dominance and status. Five years later, Jung's wife Emma wrote to Freud asking him to consider her husband as an equal,

"...Not with a father's feeling: 'He will grow and I must dwindle,' but rather as one human being thinks of another, who like you has his own law to fulfill."

Example 3: Paul Eluard, Solar Return for 1928

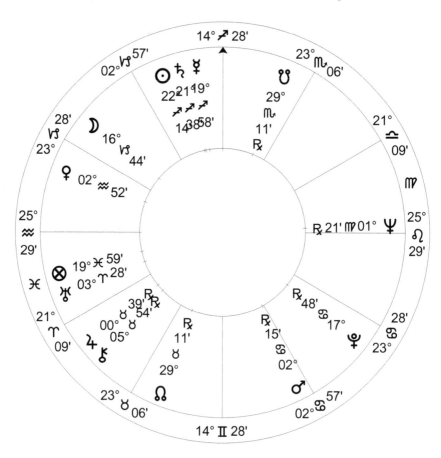

Paul Eluard
Solar return for 1928, set for birthplace

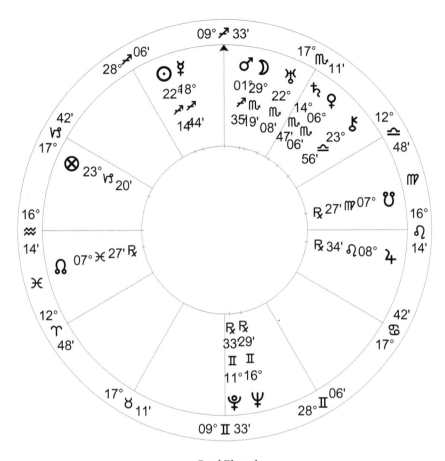

Paul Eluard
Birth Chart
December 14, 1895, 11:00 am, FROT, Saint-Denis, France

What to Look For?

Solar return Neptune is conjunct the Descendant and in the 7th house. Any transpersonal planet found in this house in the solar return will add a new dimension to relationship. We are asked to examine our dream of the other, and often we draw someone into our life who incarnates aspects of what we have always wanted - the magical, elusive prince or princess charming. We may invite another to be a touchstone to the divine and this can be disquieting and lead to errors in judgment. At the same time, Neptune is by definition a collective planet and always calls us beyond a purely individual experience. Neptune can both conjure up the dream and make it disappear in an instant. It dissolves and disperses idealized images that no longer serve us, and this can be quite painful in a marriage or another close relationship. The special veil through which we see others can be pulled away, to devastating effect. It can also correspond to a leaky feeling or a loss of energy, usually fuelled by disappointment. If we are deceived, it is often because we ask the other person to tell us what we want to hear. Here solar return Neptune is square natal Mars.

Solar return Moon is opposite Pluto, another indication of powerful experiences linked to women. In the 5th and 11th houses, this can set up a conflict between friends and lovers; one's companions might detest a new love, or there could be a situation of great passion that pulls relationships in an extreme direction, away from existing relationships. The age of thirty-three is a special year that marks the return of the Sun to it's natal house position. The solar return Ascendant is usually quite close, although it is less so here, since Aquarius is a sign of short ascension.

Solar return Sun and Mercury are conjunct here on the same degrees as natally, and in the same house, the 10th - indicating a capital year for career, for professional success, and for illuminating overall life direction. The Sun rules the 7th, so it again directs attention to relationship, to the role this plays in his life. With Saturn also involved in the conjunction, pressure is brought to bear, and events may redirect an individual against his desire. The solar return IC is very close to natal Pluto: a profound change in one's base, in security, and the home. Solar return Venus is square natal Venus, an unusual aspect peculiar to those born with the Sun close to the semi-square to Venus in the birthchart - it will repeat in the solar return every eight years. Feelings and values will be tested. Natal Venus is square Jupiter, also a repetition of a natal aspect.

What Happened?

Paul Eluard was an important figure in the surrealist movement, and one of the great French poets of the 20th century. He had met his wife Gala, in a sanatorium in Switzerland when he was sixteen; they married four years later. Gala was a tiny Russian woman with great mystique, and a muse for many of the artists in the movement. It was a rather unconventional marriage; both had lovers, and for some years Gala was also in relationship with Max Ernst. In June 1929, six months into his solar return, during a trip to Spain, Gala and Salvador Dali fell in love at first sight. She stayed with Dali for six months and returned to Eluard only to divorce. Gala became not only Dali's lover and lifelong companion, but she was also his muse and business manager for the next forty years. Dali claimed their meeting saved his life - that without Gala he might never have amounted to anything. Dali had Venus on the MC of his solar return for 1929. This is Samuel Beckett's translation of Eluard's poem, *L'Amoureuse*: [14]

> *She is standing on my lids*
> *And her hair is in my hair*
> *She has the color of my eye*
> *She has the body of my hand*
> *In my shade she is engulfed*
> *As a stone against the sky*
>
> *She will never close her eyes*
> *And she does not let me sleep*
> *And her dreams in the bright day*
> *Make the suns evaporate*
> *And me laugh cry and laugh*
> *Speak when I have nothing to say*

---

14 Samuel Beckett, "Translations of Surrealist Writings by André Breton, Paul Eluard and René Crevel," *This Quarter*, V, September 1932, pp 72-128.

Example 4: Bob Dylan, Solar Return for 1965

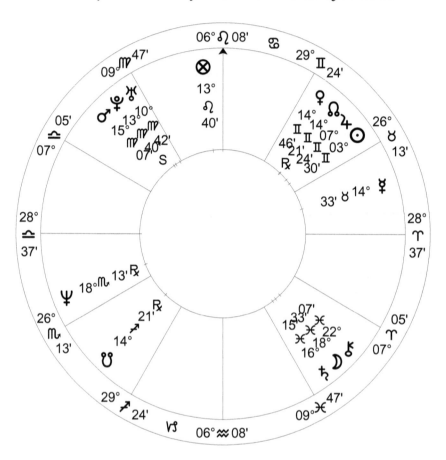

Bob Dylan
Solar return for 1965, set for birthplace

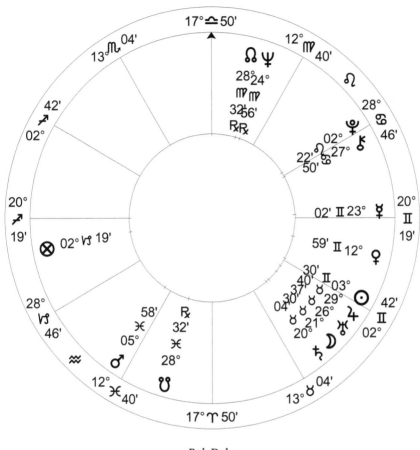

17° ♎ 50'

13° ♏ 04'

12° ♍ 40'

42' ♐ 02°

☊ ♆
28° 24°
♍ ♍
32' 56'
℞ ℞

♌
28° ♋ 46'

♇
02° ☋
22' ♌ 27° ♂
50'

20° ♐
19'

⊗ 02° ♑ 19'

02' ♊ 23° ☿
59' ♊ 12° ♀

20° ♊ 19'

28° ♑ 46'

58' ♓ 05°

℞ 32' ♓ 28°

♊
30'
40' 03°
30' 03°
04° ♉ 29° ☉
26°
♉ 21° 42'
20° ☿ ♊ 02°
♄ ♃ ♈

♒

♂

☋

12° ♓ 40'

13° ♉ 04'

17° ♈ 50'

Bob Dylan
Birth Chart
May 24, 1941, 9:05 pm, Duluth, Minnesota

What To Look For?

A striking opposition between the 5th and the 11th houses of the solar return involves six planets. Here tensions between what other people expect and what an individual chooses to do are pushed to an extreme. Given the nature of the planets involved, there is a sense of violent polarization, of friends becoming enemies, even the possibility of rejection and betrayal. An individual may choose to follow a lonely path and endure the taunts of the community. Mars-Pluto-Uranus awakens the rage of the crowd, but also reflects provocation and unpredictability. As a result, there could be a strong need to find a group of people who share one's vision of the world.

Solar return Saturn conjunct the Moon in the 5th house is a repeat of a natal aspect in the same house. This is a year where the essential meaning of the natal conjunction will be revealed. There is both a need to be in the limelight and a desire to take control of the process - love and fear, mastery and rejection. With natal Saturn in the 5th, a feeling of restriction and discomfort could accompany recognition and fame, and this is reinforced by the presence of Chiron in the solar return. There is a growing sense of increased responsibility, of the price to pay for celebrity, and the restrictions it entails. Difficulties with women, or a major commitment in love are both possibilities.

Sun conjunct Jupiter is also a repeat of a natal configuration, and will deliver on its natal promise of creative reach and adulation. In the 8th house it may bring financial rewards, but it also increases a penchant for privacy. Venus in a T-square to the 5th and 11th house planets adds complexity to relationship, love, money and sexuality, while the squares to the Moon and Pluto activate a conflict between intimacy and power. Mercury opposition Neptune across the 1st/7th axis also describes a possibility of misunderstandings, and a longing for intuitive understanding.

What Happened?

Bob Dylan was at the peak of his fame and his creative influence. His music was accelerating at an astonishing pace, changing within months of the release of a new album. As his original folk-influenced music became hugely popular, he was already shifting toward rock. Fans of his earlier folk style were horrified to hear him plug in an electric guitar at the 1965 Newport festival, and responded with vicious derision, calling him a trai-

tor and sell-out. British crowds also reacted with violence and
dislike when he toured the UK in the spring of 1966, even as he
won over new enthusiasts. In the fall of 1965, Dylan began playing with a group called the Hawks, later to be the Band, his creative collaborators for many years. He also secretly married Sara
Lowndes who became pregnant with their first child during this
solar return.

Example 5: Jenny, Solar Return for 2003

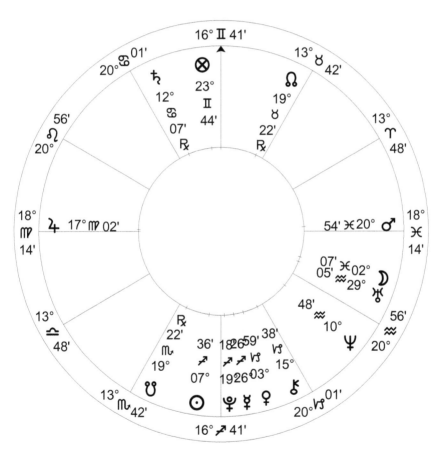

Jenny
Solar Return for 2003, set for birthplace

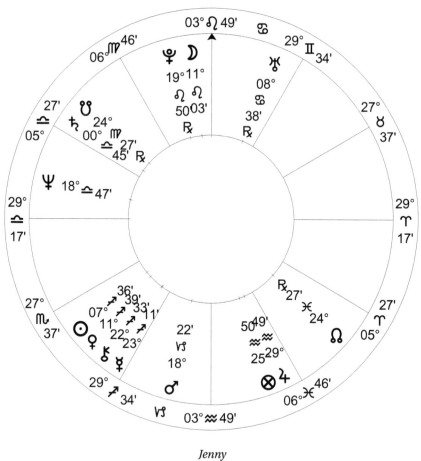

Jenny
Birth Chart
November 30, 1950, 3:40 am CST, Evansville, Indiana

What to Look For?

A dynamic T-square between Jupiter, Mars and Pluto falls on the angles of the solar return chart. The emphasis is on the 4th house of family, with Pluto on the IC conjunct Mercury and Venus not far away. There is likely to be either a physical or psychological upheaval in the family. It may involve a sudden change or acting out a struggle or conflict (Mars), and if communication has been bottled up, an incident may bring a great deal out into the open. This combination of planets could be violent or extreme in some way, and the foundation of the family will never be the same. A partner might be involved in a daring or dangerous enterprise, or could push for a permanent change, possibly with legal issues. With Jupiter on the Ascendant, she is being asked to respond generously and confidently to another's provocation. Pluto and Mars are almost exactly square – they signal an issue with extreme willfulness, and possible power struggles.

Solar Return Moon is conjunct Uranus in the 6th house, another indicator for sudden change, possibly affecting work or health. The Moon in Pisces is very full; emotions can come rushing in, whether they are difficult or ecstatic. The dam bursts and there is a sense of fragility, an inability to keep out the sea of feelings, whether they are one's own or someone else's. Uranus is on the degree of natal Jupiter, which amplifies and releases the conjunction.

What Happened?

Jenny's elderly father, a remarkable man with a gift for business, had organized a secure financial future for his daughters. Horrified at the idea of losing his independence, and fearing a stroke, he took a gun and shot himself in the head. His octogenarian wife found the body in his upstairs bedroom. Jenny, in a state of profound shock, flew in to help her mother and sisters with the clean up, and all the practical details that had been left behind. She was profoundly unsettled by her father's sudden, violent death for many months, and there was a great deal of communication between the siblings (Sun in the 3rd house). He committed suicide on February 4, 2004, two months and a few days after her birthday. Pluto is a little over two degrees from the IC, and Mars is two and a half degrees from the Descendant; their energies are reinforced by the square.

Example 6: Antoine de Saint-Exupéry, Solar Return for 1942

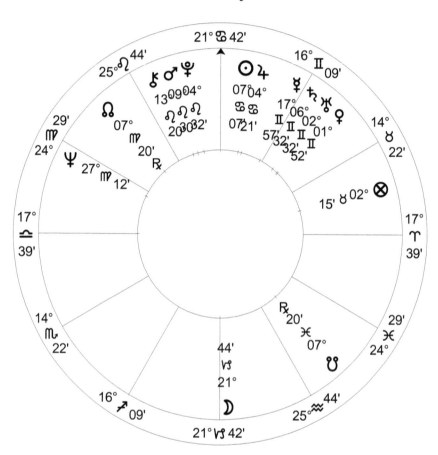

Antoine de Saint-Exupéry
Solar Return for 1942, set for birthplace

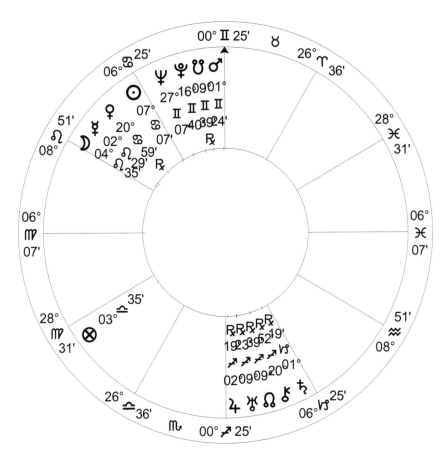

Antoine de Saint-Exupéry
Birth Chart
June 29, 1900, 9:15 am FROT Lyon, France

What to Look For

An exalted Jupiter is conjunct the Sun in the 9th house of the solar return, bringing recognition for understanding, knowledge or wisdom. The 9th house allows knowledge to be disseminated on the widest possible scale, unlimited by time or geography. It connects us to a sense of higher purpose, to questions of meaning, and we may be asked to step into the role of expert, guide, or teacher. Or we could be moved to learn about other cultures or philosophies and meet those who can be our guides, who can open our eyes to the world in a new way.

Solar return Moon in Capricorn is conjunct the IC. Emotionally, the Moon pulls us toward the past or makes us aware of the need for security. Moon in earth brings a desire for measurable results. In Capricorn, there may be emotional frustration or a great sense of responsibility. Moon is on the Sun/Mars midpoint: a call to action.

Transiting Pluto is exactly conjunct the natal Moon, reflected by Pluto's position in the solar return. There is a need to break with the way things have been, an emotional point of no return. Collective energies are building and may become a key part of the year. These are times when an individual can be swept away or asked to step into a high-profile role. Mars-Pluto-Chiron in the 10th house indicates a struggle of some kind, an extreme response to authority, even at great cost to oneself. Linked to the natal Moon, a rush to defend the vulnerable is likely.

An 8th house conjunction of Venus, Uranus and Saturn, brings almost unbearable tension and a need for change. Relationships could be strained. Solar return Venus and Uranus are conjunct natal Mars and MC. This combination brings passion, and life is run with the heart in a way that is visible to others, attracting and generating love. Uranus adds wildness, reactivity, an urgent push for change, or a need for risk. Solar return Mercury is conjunct natal Pluto - a tendency to disappear from sight in order to spend time, locked in the "alchemical lab," confronting difficult or hidden subjects.

What Happened?

Saint-Exupéry had become a best-selling author in the United States when *Flight to Arras* was published in English the previous year. Despite this, he keenly felt his position as an exile in New York, and great frustration at his inability to fight in the war against the Germans. *The Little Prince*, his best-loved book, was published in April 1943. Originally intended for children, it has become a classic fable, translated into a hundred languages, with over thirty-four million copies sold. Around the same time, Saint-Exupéry eagerly answered the call to fly planes in North Africa for the Free French.

Example Seven: Mia Farrow, Solar Returns for 1991 and 1992

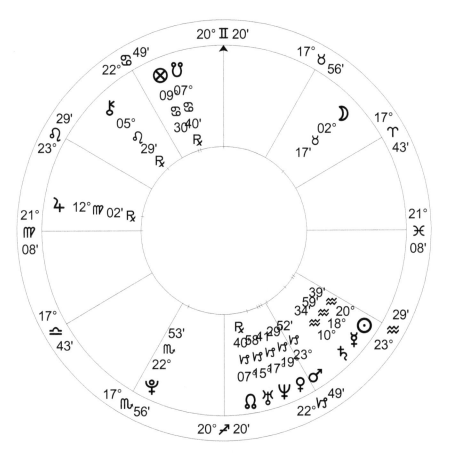

Mia Farrow
Solar Return for 1992, set for birthplace

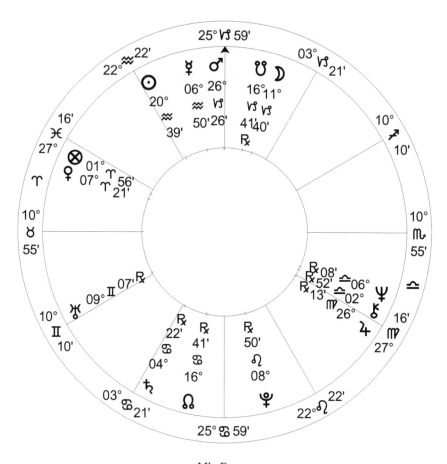

Mia Farrow
Birth Chart
February 9, 1945, 11:27 am PWT, Los Angeles, California

What to Look For?

Age forty-seven brings Mars back to its natal position in the solar return, emphasizing achievement and triumph, struggle or conflict. It's a good idea to check Mars in the natal chart – it's house will often give an idea of what area in life will be affected. In her birth chart, Mia Farrow has an exalted Mars in Capricorn conjunct the MC. In the solar return for 1992, the Sun in Aquarius is closely square Pluto; the transit is in effect, so this is a period that may bring a profound change in identity, affecting relationships with men. There may be a period where she is overshadowed by powerful events.

The solar return Moon in the 8th asks us to look at the less savory aspects of our feeling life; it echoes Plutonian themes of crisis, transformation, sexuality, death and betrayal, the realm of secrets and hidden feelings. A strong conjunction of Neptune, Uranus, Venus and Mars evokes change, excitement, passion, and upset in relationship. In the 4th house, it points to a family crisis. It conjuncts the natal south Node, adding a note of compulsion, and possible renunciation. A strong 4th and 5th house emphasis suggests a year centering around family and children, awakening issues from the past. Mars in the 5th suggests a battle with or for a child.

The solar return Ascendant falls in the natal 5th house pointing again to children. It is six degrees from natal Jupiter. Jupiter can give a sense of righteousness. Solar return Saturn picks up a natal opposition between Mercury and Pluto, emphasizing the need to communicate head-on about difficult themes. The solar return relocated for New York, Farrow's place of residence, gives Chiron on the MC and Moon on the Descendant, bringing out an image of the wronged and wounded woman and mother, revealing her emotions to the world.

What Happened?

This is the year a huge public scandal blasted apart a long personal and working relationship between Mia Farrow and Woody Allen. Mia had discovered Allen's affair with her 17-year-old daughter Soon Yi the previous year, with Uranus and Neptune conjunct the solar return Descendant (see 1991 solar return chart below). She went to "war" in 1992, filing charges accusing Allen of abusing their adopted daughter Dylan. He counter-sued for custody. A highly public and acrimonious scandal damaged Allen's reputation and splintered their relationship for good. It was also a professional split, and Mia's career went into a lower gear.

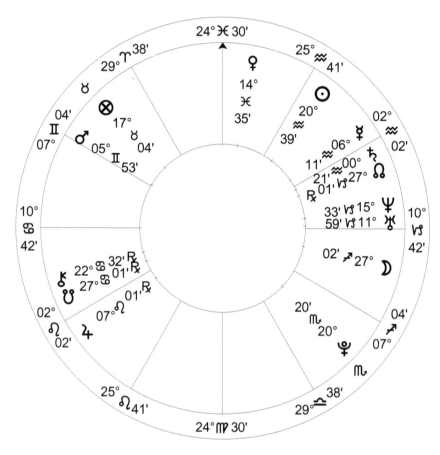

Mia Farrow
Solar Return for 1991, set for birthplace

What to Look For

Uranus is tightly conjunct the Descendant with a one-degree orb signaling a shake-up in relationship. There is a strong possibility for reversals, for surprise and sudden change involving partners. Uranus is conjunct Neptune; the shock could be followed by a period of sadness or disillusionment, loss and vulnerability. The need to break apart old models of relating is strong, but at odds with Saturn and the north Node. Relationships may never be the same. The Descendant is also conjunct the natal Moon, highlighting the importance of emotions. The solar return IC is conjunct natal Jupiter, asking her to look within for healing.

There is an exact Mercury return. These years always emphasize our perception, our ability to see what is happening. Mercury opposition Jupiter overlays a natal Mercury opposition Pluto. In the 8th house of secrets, and opposing Jupiter, there could be a revelation of some kind - Jupiter brings things into the open and heightens the effect whatever natal planet it contacts. Conjunct natal Pluto, Jupiter brings the muck up to the surface.

The solar return Moon in a fire sign is unaspected. Any unaspected planet can either dominate the year or disappear from view – it is unrestrained and unintegrated, a wild card. Fire indicates a willingness to take risks. In the 6th, there is work to be done, the image of the feminine could be devalued. The Sun is exactly square Pluto, an ongoing transit: an underworld initiation, an encounter with the dark side of the masculine image, and through that encounter a profound change in self awareness. Sun in the 8th square Pluto in the 5th concerns sexuality and passion.

Uranus is in a partile conjunction to the natal Moon, bringing freedom from childhood patterns, asking her to step out from the caretaker role. This aspect reflects the exact Uranus-Moon transit, signaling that it is time to step away from the past. It is a time of great insecurity, or intense excitement.

What Happened

Mia Farrow found nude photos of her adopted daughter Soon-Yi in Woody Allen's apartment. A huge crisis ensued. Hoping for a reconciliation after the crisis, she continued to work with Allen on *Husbands and Wives*, a film about the collapse of a marriage.

Example Eight: Annie, Solar Return for 2003

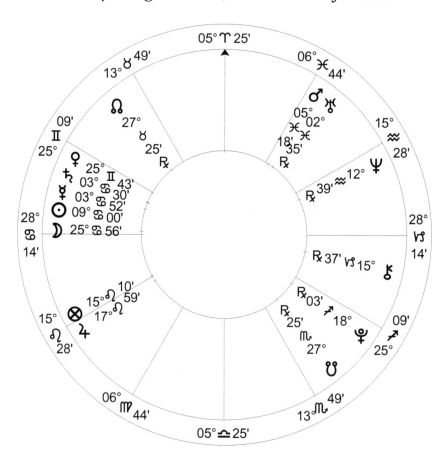

Annie
Solar Return for 2003, set for birthplace

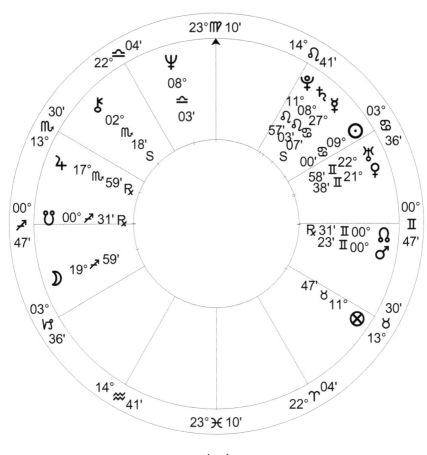

Annie
Birth Chart
July 1, 1947, 5:50 PM MET, Paris, France

What to Look For

The solar return Moon is conjunct the Ascendant in its own sign, Cancer. This is a year when long-held-back emotions may emerge into the foreground. The past will influence the present. Feelings will take priority. There is a sense of renewal linked to the new Moon phase. A powerful emphasis on the water element reinforces the primacy of feeling.

A strong 12th house suggests a reactivation of past cycles in the current solar return. There may be an alternative explanation of one's personal narrative (Mercury-Saturn). Any communication will have a profound effect.

Solar return Mars and Uranus conjunct in the 8th indicates the need to break out, to confront taboos, or to be sexually alive. Its trine to 12th house planets emphasizes something hidden from others and yet deeply meaningful. It brings energy and unpredictability to the past. The solar return Ascendant falls in the natal 8th house of secrets and sexuality. It is conjunct natal Mercury, bringing hidden (natal 8th house) thoughts and feelings out into the open. Solar return Pluto is conjunct the natal Moon, a once-in-a-lifetime transit that brings the possibility of rebirth, death and transformation. It also aspects natal Venus, bringing a complete redefinition of herself as a woman. Solar return Venus is conjunct natal Uranus, reinforcing the freedom-loving and erotic element of the solar return Mars-Uranus. It is opposite a 5th house Pluto in the solar return, suggesting a heightening of passion or obsession as the year unfolds. The solar return IC conjuncts natal Neptune: coming home to a dream or an ideal.

What Happened

A few months before this solar return, Annie began communicating with a former lover, a man she'd left to marry her husband thirty years before. They spoke of their unchanged feelings for each other, and just after her birthday, they met in a foreign country and began a passionate affair. This was experienced as a renewal of a soul connection, a powerful lifelong love relationship. They were separated by geography and professional commitments. She was married to an older man and unwilling to abandon him, so the relationship remained secret. She also purchased a country home, a place linked to many childhood memories.

Example Nine: François, Solar Return for 2000

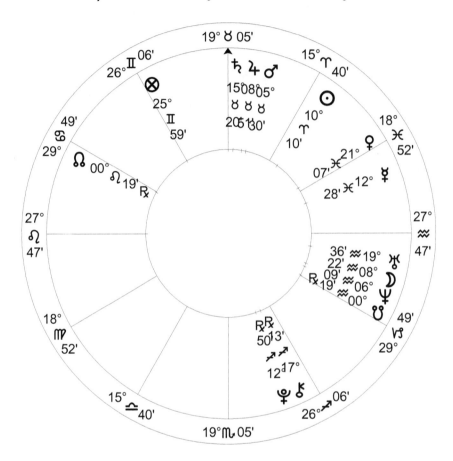

François
Solar return for 2000, set for birthplace

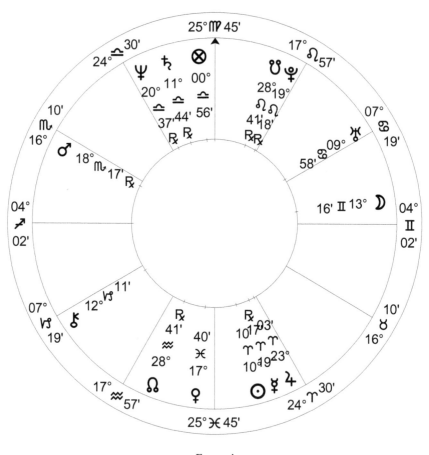

François
Birth Chart
March 30, 1952, 11:52 pm, Chalon-sur-Saône, France

What to Look For

A strong 6th house emphasis in the solar return chart with the
Moon conjunct Neptune and the south node could indicate an
emphasis on health or illness. This could involve sudden drops
or leaks in energy. A woman may play a particular role as caretaker or helper, or there can be a need to work on relationships
with women. Solar return Saturn is conjunct the Midheaven, signaling a year of consequence, one of heightened responsibility,

or a moral dilemma. From the 9th house side it may test one's beliefs, one's faith in life.

The Moon is exactly square Jupiter and only three degrees from a square to Mars, giving a feeling of excitement, of excess, extra effort. Three planets in the 6th house square three planets in the 9th house, giving a sense of things speeding up, of physical and mental stimulation, travel for work, or a project requiring an unusual effort.

The solar return Ascendant in Leo conjuncts the natal South Node, signaling a year of emptying out. Its ruler, the Sun, is in the 8th house of crisis. The solar return Ascendant falls in the natal 9th house, emphasizing travel, philosophy, ethics, teaching, belief systems, or religion. Solar return Pluto opposes the natal Moon, an ongoing transit that is likely to change the significant relationships in his life, to shake up his marriage and other relationships with women, and to bring issues of dependency to a head. The solar return IC is on the degree of natal Mars in Scorpio, an urgent, shot-out-of-a-gun signature: the need for intense and rapid action, survival and defense.

What Happened?

About five months after his birthday, while walking in the hills with a friend, he was overcome by intense fatigue. His heart had sped up and he was losing consciousness. He was helped down the mountain and airlifted by helicopter to the hospital; he had a near-death experience, an out-of-body journey. He had to stop working, and recovered slowly with a pacemaker. His philosophy changed, his heart opened: he had a hard look at his marriage and decided to separate. He divorced a few years later, and while exploring the psychological factors underlying his heart problems, began working with the language of the body and how it encodes family inheritance and emotional beliefs.

Example Ten: Sandra K., Lunar Return for February 2004

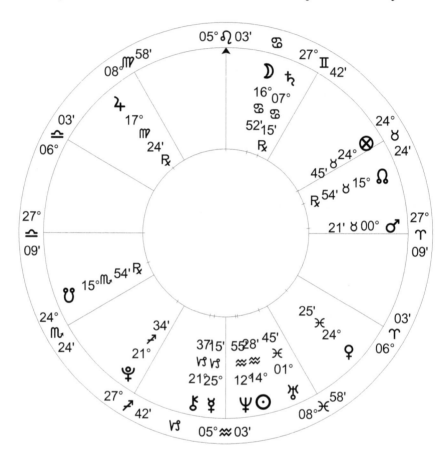

Sandra K.
Lunar return February 2004, set for birthplace

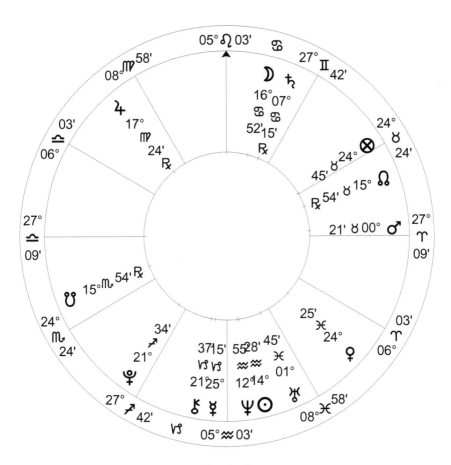

Sandra K.
Lunar return February 2004, relocated for Paris, France

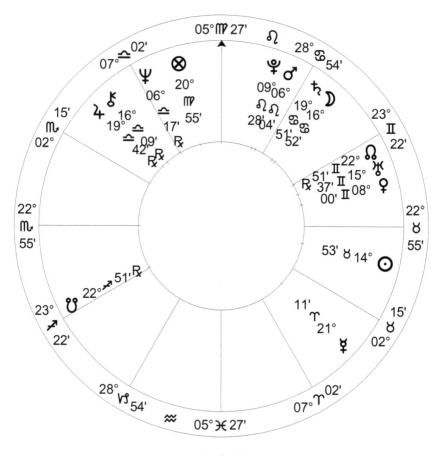

Sandra K.
Birth Chart
May 5, 1946, 8:32 pm EDT, New York, New York

What to Look For?

Uranus is angular, conjunct the Descendant, signaling a sudden shift in relationship. It may bring a new person into our lives, or an unexpected event in an existing relationship. Surprise is the order of the day, and we become aware that human beings can be wildly unpredictable, that life has a trajectory independent of our desires or wishes. Uranus can also bring experiences of synchronicity, of sudden illumination or discovery. In the 7th house, this experience of discovery includes other people. Uranus is one degree from the Descendant, drawing our attention to the time immediately following this lunar return.

Leo is on the Ascendant, bringing a natally-intercepted sign onto the angles of the lunar return chart. Normally less accessible due to its natal interception, the Leo/Aquarius axis falls across the natal 3rd/9th houses, heightening issues of awareness, understanding, and communication. The Moon is in a partile trine and sextile to the lunar Nodes, often connected to some kind of fated experience. The Moon is also sextile Jupiter.

Relocated Lunar Return

In the relocated lunar return, Neptune is on the IC, an aspect of nostalgia, of imaginative connection to a spiritual home, to a dream of emotional healing. Mars is conjunct the Descendant, signaling that other people will have enormous impact and will initiate movement in relationship. It could also bring a struggle of some kind.

What Happened?

Her brother called to say he had been found by their long lost mother after over fifty years without contact. Sandra spoke to her mother for the first time on February 4, the day after this lunar return - one of the most extraordinary moments of her life. This first conversation immediately broke through a lifetime of unknowing, instantly changing her perception of the past. She learned of the existence of her half-sister and spoke to her for the first time. Her son had left for university many thousands of miles away just one month before, unknowingly moving to a place a few hours' drive from her newly found mother and sister.

Example Eleven: Martha Stewart, Lunar Return for December 2001

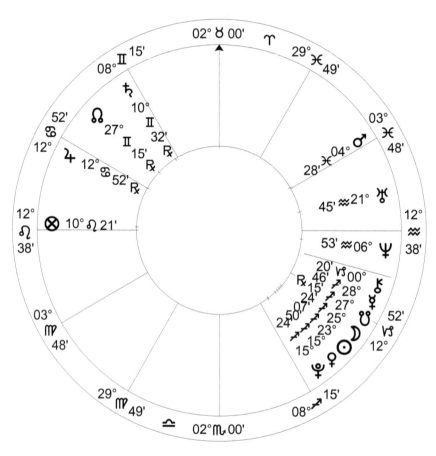

Martha Stewart
Lunar return for December 2001, set for birthplace

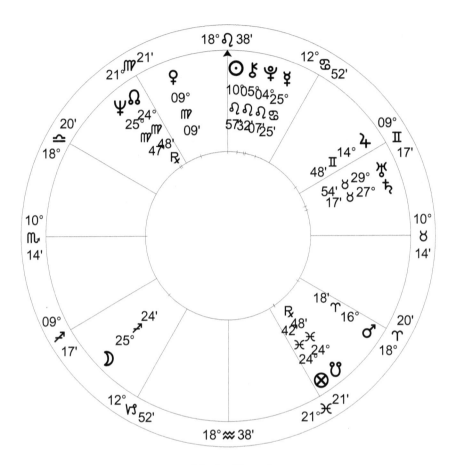

Martha Stewart
August 3, 1941, 1:33 pm, Jersey City, New Jersey

What to Look For?

An extremely potent stellium and solar eclipse falls in the 5th house of the lunar return. The 5th house has a great deal to do with our presentation self, the image we offer to others in order to draw their attention, appreciation and love. An eclipse in this house, with its image of a shadow passing over the disk of the Sun, gives a striking symbol for the shadow that entered Stewart's life during this time. The 5th house rules speculation and risk; it is a house of games, of delight, of children or childlike behavior. Again, all of this becomes fraught with consequence given the presence of an eclipse.

Venus is exactly conjunct Pluto, an aspect that indicates an extreme of feeling or desire, the possibility of being possessed or taken over, of falling into compulsive behavior. This could easily symbolize a dangerous liaison, a headstrong affair, with almost tragic consequences. Neptune is widely conjunct the Descendant from the 6th house, which could indicate unsound or unclear counsel from employees. Uranus in the 7th may bring a change in relationships.

What Happened?

This is the lunar return for the sale of Martha Stewart's ImClone stocks. Acting on a tip from her broker to sell before the release of an unfavorable report by the FDA, Martha broke the law. The insider trading scandal that broke out consumed her life for the next four years and ultimately sent her to jail for five months. Not only did her reputation suffer, but the value of her business was hurt by the scandal, and she had to resign as head of her company.

BIBLIOGRAPHY

Astrological References

Bell, Lynn. "Your Annual Birthday Chart: Solar Returns Explained", *The Mountain Astrologer,* Aug/Sep 1999

Bell, Lynn. "Rudhyar et les Révolutions Solaires", Actes du Congres ARRC/RAH Paris 1995

Brady, Bernadette. *The Eagle and the Lark,* York Beach, ME: Samuel Weiser 1992

Costello, Darby. *Water and Fire,* Raven Dreams Press, Boulder, CO, 2019 (CPA Press, 1998)

Costello, Darby. *Earth and Air,* Raven Dreams Press, Boulder, CO, 2018 (CPA Press, 1999)

Eshelman, James. *Interpreting Solar Returns,* San Diego: ASC Publications 1986 (Astro-Analytic Publications, 1979)

Greene, Liz. *Relating: An Astrological Guide to Living with Others,* Northamptonshire, UK: The Aquarian Press, 1990 (1977)

Greene, Liz & Saspotas, Howard. *The Luminaries,* York Beach, ME: Samuel Weiser 1992

Harding, Michael & Charles Harvey. *Working with Astrology*, London: Arkana, 1990

Kirby, Babs & Janey Stubbs. *Interpreting Solar & Lunar Returns, a Psychological Approach*, Longmean, Shaftesbury, Dorset: Element Books Limited, 1990

March, Marion D. & Joan McEvers. *The Only Way to Learn about Tomorrow*, San Diego: ASC Publications, 1988

Merriman, Raymond A. *The Solar Return Book of Prediction*, Birmingham, MI: Seek It Publications, 1977

Shea, Mary. *Planets in Solar Returns*, San Diego: ASC Publications, 1992.

Volguine, Alexandre. *La Technique des Révolutions Solaires*, Paris: Dervy Livres, 1988 (1936).

Biographical References

Beckett, Samuel. *"Translations of Surrealist Writings"* par BRETON (André), Eluard (Paul) et Crevel (René), *This Quarter, V,* September 1932, pp. 72-128

Corliss, Richard & Jeffrey Ressner. "Peter Pan Grows Up, But Can He Still Fly?", *Time Magazine*, May 19, 1997

Dylan, Bob. *Chronicles, Vol I*, New York: Simon and Schuster, 2004

Farrow, Mia. *What Falls Away*, New York: Random House, 1997

Jung, C.G. *Memories, Dreams, and Reflections*, New York: Pantheon Books, 1973

Kadlec, Daniel. "Not a Good thing for Martha", Time Magazine, March 15, 2004

McGuire, William, ed. *The Freud Jung Letters: The Correspondence Between Sigmund Freud and C.G. Jung* (abridged paperback edition), Princeton: Princeton University Press 1994

Munson, Richard. *Cousteau: The Captain and His World*, New York: William Morrow & Co., 1989

Plotz, David. "Martha Stewart: She's a Good Thing", *Slate Magazine*, retrieved October 22, 1999, at 6:00 pm, https://slate.com/news-and-politics/1999/10/martha-stewart.html

Thottam, Jyoti. "Why They're Picking on Martha", *Time Magazine*, June 6, 2003

Rudhyar Archival Project, "Dane Rudhyar: An Illustrated Biographical Sketch", http://www.khaldea.com/rudhyar/bio1.shtml

Rudhyar, Dane. *Dane Rudhyar: His Life and Works*, "To Sow", Special Catalog Edition, 1989

http://www.alalettre.com/eluard.php

https://www.antoinedesaintexupery.com/

https://www.alalettre.com/saint-exupery.php

Chart Sources

Deborah, Claire and Katia presented their birth data during the seminar. All private case histories use data from birth records.

Annie, July 1, 1947, 5:50 pm MET (16:50 GMT), Paris, France

Claire, January 19, 1961, 2:44 pm (11:44 GMT), Nakuru, Kenya

Ellen, February 4, 1961, 12:10 pm MET (11:50 GMT), Paris, France

Francois, March 30, 1952, 11:52 pm MET (22:52 GMT), Chalon-sur-Saône, France

Janice, October 15, 1938, 2:45 am EST (07:45 GMT), New Haven, Connecticut

Jeff, May 16, 1946, 7:35 am GMT, New York, New York

Jenny, November 30, 1950, 3:40 am CST (09:40 GMT) , Evans-ville, Indiana

Katia, January 31, 1970, 1:10 am MET (00:10 am GMT), Belgrade, Serbia

Sandra K., May 5, 1946, 8:32 pm EDT (00:32 GMT on May 6), New York, New York

Thalia, July 19, 1958, 4:45 am MET (3:45 GMT), Tunis, Tunisia

Jacques-Yves Cousteau, June 11, 1910, 1:15 pm FROT (13:06 GMT), Saint-André-de-Cubzac, France. Source: Astrodatabank, AA-rated. Note: many sources give a spelling error for birthplace, citing Saint-André-de-Cubzac.

Bob Dylan, May 24, 1941, 9:05 pm CST (03:05 GMT on May 25), Duluth, Minnesota. Source: Astrodatabank, AA-rated.

Paul Éluard, December 14, 1895, 11:00 am FROT (10:51 GMT), Saint-Denis, France. Source: Astrodatabank, AA-rated.

Mia Farrow, February 9, 1945, 11:27 am PWT (18:27 GMT), Los Angeles, California. Source: Astrodatabank, AA-rated.

Sigmund Freud, May 6, 1856, 6:30 pm LMT (17:17 GMT), Freiberg, Moravia (now Príbor, Czech Republic). Source: Astrodatabank, AA-rated.

Carl Gustav Jung, July 26, 1875, 7:32 pm SZOT (19:02 GMT), Kesswill, Switzerland. Source: Astrodatabank, C-rated.

Dane Rudhyar, March 23, 1895, 12:42 am LMT (00:33 GMT), Paris, France. Source: Astrodatabank, alternate rectified time. "Leyla Rael quotes him, rectified by him to 0:42 a.m. from a given time of midnight to 1:00 AM."

Antoine de Saint-Exupéry, June 29, 1900, 9:15 am FROT (09:06 GMT), Lyon, France. Source: Astrodatabank, AA-rated.

Steven Spielberg, December 18, 1946, 6:16 pm EST (23:16 GMT), Cincinnati, Ohio. Source: Astrodatabank, AA-rated.

Martha Stewart, August 3, 1941, 1:33 pm EDT (17:33 GMT), Jersey City, New Jersey. Source: Astrodatabank, AA-rated.

Ingram Content Group UK Ltd.
Milton Keynes UK
UKHW020810150323
418604UK00014B/1473